Edexcel GCE History

Britain and Ireland 1867–1922

Martin Collier

Series editors: Martin Collier   Rosemary Rees

Unit 2 Student Book

A PEARSON COMPANY

Heinemann is an imprint of Pearson Education Limited, a company incorporated in England and Wales, having its registered office at Edinburgh Gate, Harlow, Essex, CM20 2JE. Registered company number: 872828

www.heinemann.co.uk

Heinemann is a registered trademark of Pearson Education Limited

Text © Martin Collier 2008

First published 2008

12 11 10 09 08

10 9 8 7 6 5 4 3 2 1

British Library Cataloguing in Publication Data is available from the British Library on request.

ISBN 978 0 435308 27 8

Edited, designed, typeset and produced by Florence Production Ltd, Stoodleigh, Devon

Original illustrations © Pearson Education Ltd 2008

Cover design by Siu Hang Wong

Picture research by Zooid Pictures

Printed in the UK by Scotprint

Acknowledgements

The author and publisher would like to thank the following individuals and organisations for permission to reproduce photographs:

p.2 © Alamy / The Print Collector; p.6 © Alamy / Classic Image; p.8 © Alamy / Mary Evans Picture Library; p.13 © Alamy / The Print Collector; p.19 © Alamy / Lordprice Collection; p.19 © Alamy / Lordprice Collection; p.31 © Alamy / Mary Evans Picture Library; p.33 © Alamy / The Print Collector; p.43 © Library of Congress; p.44 © Alamy / The Print Collector; p.45 (top) © Alamy / Mary Evans Picture Library; p.45 (bottom) © Mary Evans Picture Library; p.46 © Alamy / The Print Collector; p.53 © Alamy / The Print Collector; p.57 © Alamy / Mary Evans Picture Library; p.61 © Mary Evans Picture Library; p.67 © Punch; p.68 © Mary Evans Picture Library; p.70 © National Library of Ireland; p.72 © National Library of Ireland; p.73 © Mary Evans Picture Library; p.74 © Punch; p.76 © Punch; p.88 © Photographers Direct / LordPrice Collection; p.90 © Getty / Hulton Archive; p.92 © Corbis / Hulton Archive; p.96 © Linenhall Library; p.101 © Getty / Hulton Archive; p.107 © National Library of Ireland; p.113 © National Library of Ireland; p.115 © National Library of Ireland; p.116 © Mary Evans Picture Library; p.122 © Alamy / The Print Collector; p.124 © Mary Evans Picture Library / Illustrated London News Ltd; p.125 © National Library of Ireland; p.131 © Punch; p.135 © National Library of Ireland; p.142 © Getty / Hulton Archive; p.144 © Alamy / Mary Evans Picture Library; p.147 © Crawford Municipal Art Gallery, Cork, Ireland; p.150 © Punch; p.155 © Punch; p.161 © Corbis

Every effort has been made to contact copyright holders of material reproduced in this book. Any omissions will be rectified in subsequent printings if notice is given to the publishers.

Websites
The websites used in this book were correct and up-to-date at the time of publication. It is essential for tutors to preview each website before using it in class so as to ensure that the URL is still accurate, relevant and appropriate. We suggest that tutors bookmark useful websites and consider enabling students to access them through the school/college intranet.

Dedication
To my mother.

Contents

Introduction

The Troubles

At 2.54am on 12 October 1984 a bomb ripped through the heart of the Grand Hotel in Brighton. The bomb had been planted by Patrick Magee, a member of a terrorist organisation known as the Irish Republican Army (IRA). At the time, Britain had a Conservative government and they were meeting in Conference in Brighton. Staying at the hotel on the night of the explosion was the British Prime Minister Mrs Margaret Thatcher, many Cabinet ministers and leading members of the Conservative Party. Magee had booked into the hotel in mid-September and had planted the bomb with a delayed timer set to go off 24 days later. Mrs Thatcher and the Cabinet ministers staying at the hotel escaped serious injury. However, five people were killed and 34 were injured.

Those murdered and those injured by the bomb represented a fraction of those killed and maimed in the period of violence known as The Troubles which lasted from roughly the late 1960s to the late 1990s. Most of those who died in The Troubles were killed in Northern Ireland but the violence spread to mainland Britain and southern Ireland. Many of those who died were innocent victims of what is known as sectarian violence; violence of one sect or group within society against another. In Northern Ireland, the main sectarian division was between those who were mainly Catholics and wanted a united Ireland that was independent of British rule, and those who were mainly Protestants and wanted to be part of Britain. The violence of The Troubles was seemingly endless as was the sadness and despair.

The Troubles was just one violent period of many which litter Irish history.

Peace

There were many on both sides of the Irish Sea who wished to find a peaceful way forward and an end to the violence of The Troubles. On 10th April 1998 an agreement known as the Good Friday Agreement was signed in Belfast. The agreement set out a path for peace and closer agreement and collaboration between the governments of Britain and Ireland. It also set out a timetable for the terrorist organisations involved in the violence to lay down their weapons. The price for peace was a high one, as terrorist organisations demanded the release of their members who had been tried and convicted of violent actions and were serving often lengthy prison sentences in jail, as part of the conditions for laying down their arms. In June 1999 Patrick Magee was released from prison after serving only 14 years of a life sentence. The pendulum of Irish history had again swung away from violence and in favour of those who wished to find a peaceful way ahead through constitutional means.

In May 2007, one of the architects of the Good Friday Agreement and the then Taoiseach (Prime Minister) of the Republic of Ireland, Bertie Ahern, addressed both Houses of Parliament in Westminster. He was the first Taoiseach ever to do so. In his speech the Taoiseach dwelt on the past and present relationship between Britain and Ireland. In so doing he identified many of the themes that run through this book.

Mr Ahern accurately summarized the relationship between Britain and Ireland as being 'old and extraordinary' as well as being 'close, complex and difficult'.

He highlighted Irishmen from the past who had sought to seek improvement for Ireland through peaceful means.

> For over two centuries, great Irishmen came to Westminster to be a voice for the voiceless of Ireland and at times a conscience for Britain too. I am thinking above all of Daniel O'Connell and of Charles Stewart Parnell, but the tradition is long and noble. And their struggle to further the cause of the Irish nation in this parliament resonated across the Irish Sea through the lives of every Irish person.

An important theme that runs thorough this book is the deep division in Ireland between the two political traditions of nationalism and unionism. In his speech Mr Ahern tried to explain how the two traditions might be reconciled: 'Irish nationalism has its heroes as does unionism. We need to acknowledge each others' pride in our separate and divided past.'

One thing about Irish history is that nothing is ever clear cut. While as many Irish people at the beginning of the twentieth century wished to see the end of British rule, so many did not. Mr Ahern recognised that many Irish people were loyal to the British Crown and, when war broke out in 1914, were prepared to fight for Britain. He spoke of the '200,000 young men from across the island of Ireland, Catholic and Protestant, North and South, who fought in the First World War, side by side' and their 'spirit of an imperishable heroism'.

There are other themes that were mentioned by Mr Ahern in his speech that will be discussed in this book. He pointed out that 'no two nations and no two peoples have closer ties of history and geography and of family and friendship' because of the large scale migration from Ireland to Britain over the centuries. He also highlighted the rich cultural and trading links between the two islands.

> One of the most creative moments in human history was the meeting between the English language and the Irish people. It has given us some of the great works of world literature – of Jonathan Swift, Oscar Wilde,

James Joyce, George Bernard Shaw, William Butler Yeats, Samuel Beckett, John McGahern and many, many others . . . They all found their genius in the English language, but they drew on a perspective that was uniquely Irish.

The story of Irish history is one of tragedy and sorrow, of triumph and of disaster. The period covered by this book is perhaps more dramatic than any other. At the heart of the book is the relationship between Britain and Ireland and the divisions within Ireland about how that relationship might develop. Despite numerous attempts at a peaceful settlement, the book tells the story of missed opportunity, bad luck and violence. Although sad, this is a story which needs to be told, as Mr Ahern said in his speech:

> We cannot look back through eras far removed from the standards and promise of today, through the very pages of our common past, and tear out the bloodstained chapters. But that does not mean we should write them into the story of our future. Violence is part of our shared past that lasted too long. Now we close the chapter, we move on, and it will remain there as it was written.

There has not been enough space in this introduction to give an alternative point of view to that of Mr Ahern's. Given his audience, Mr Ahern's comments were friendly and measured. However, some might have disagreed with a number of his remarks. As the leader of the Republic of Ireland, he has put his spin on Irish history, just as a unionist or someone British might have a very different point of view. Another aim of this book is to look critically at the evidence as provided by both those who lived through it, and by historians themselves. The book hopes to stimulate debate and discussion which will lead to a better understanding of the history of Ireland in the period in question.

1 The Irish question

What is this unit about?

This unit focuses on the main themes that run through the study of Ireland in the period 1867–1922. In this unit you will:

- find out about how, from the Act of Union of 1801, Ireland was ruled as part of Britain. You will also find out how many people, called unionists, supported the union of Britain and Ireland;
- discover how others, known as nationalists, wanted Ireland to rule itself and how two different strands of nationalism developed; constitutional nationalism (working within the political system for change) and revolutionary nationalism (working outside the political system);
- find out about the role played by individuals, including Daniel O'Connell, and the significance of events such as the Great Famine.

Key questions

- How did Irish nationalism and unionism develop in the first half of the nineteenth century?
- What were the key issues that defined Irish politics and culture?

Timeline

1798	Rebellion of the Society of United Irishmen led by Wolfe Tone is crushed at the battle of Vinegar Hill in June
1800	The Act of Union joins Britain and Ireland, as from 1 January 1801
1820s	Secret society unrest led by groups such as the Whiteboys
1823	Catholic Association founded by Daniel O'Connell
1829	The Catholic Emancipation Act allowing Catholics to enter parliament and to hold public office
1830	Tithe War breaks out
1838	Tithes are reduced by 25 per cent
1840	Young Ireland is founded
1845–49	The Great Famine kills around 1 million Irish

The Union

The first invasion of Ireland from England took place in 1169. For the next 650 years the relationship between Ireland and England (and then Britain) was often violent and always difficult. By the terms of the 1801 Act of Union, Ireland and Great Britain were united into the United Kingdom.

Look at this cartoon from ***Punch*** **magazine**. The cartoon is a piece of **satire**.

Source A

PUNCH, OR THE LONDON CHARIVARI.—March 3, 1866.

REBEL [ ] ION

THE FENIAN-PEST.

Hibernia. "O MY DEAR SISTER, WHAT *ARE* WE TO DO WITH THESE TROUBLESOME PEOPLE?"
Britannia. "TRY ISOLATION FIRST, MY DEAR, AND THEN———"

1.1 *The Fenian Pest* by John Tenniel, published in *Punch* magazine in 1866.

Definitions

***Punch* magazine**

Punch magazine was set up in 1841 by Henry Mayhew. Within a decade it had become very popular, especially among the middle classes because it was sophisticated rather than rude in its humour.

Satire

is the use of humour or irony to make a point.

Discussion points

Before you read any further discuss these points with others in your discussion group:

- What are the messages of this cartoon about the relationship between Britain and Ireland?
- How representative is this cartoon of British attitudes towards Ireland?

Once you have discussed these points, compare your thoughts with other discussion groups.

Biography

John Tenniel (1820–1914)

John Tenniel was one of the most famous illustrators of his age, indeed he drew the pictures for the first edition of Lewis Carroll's *Alice's Adventures in Wonderland*. He joined *Punch* after its lead illustrator Richard Doyle left in protest over the magazine's anti-Catholic attitude. In 1864 Tenniel became head illustrator at *Punch*. In this role he drew some of the most memorable pictures of the Victorian Age. His ability to summarise popular attitudes in cartoons gained him the respect of Victorian society and in 1893 he was knighted by Queen Victoria.

It is clear from this cartoon that, in 1866, there was tension in the relationship between Britain and Ireland. Hibernia (another word for Ireland) seems frightened of the **Fenian** threat. Britannia seems to suggest that, if isolation does not work, then harsher measures will follow. The artist who drew this cartoon for *Punch* was John Tenniel. In answering how representative this picture is, you may have come to the conclusion that this is just the view of the artist. However, such a conclusion would not be entirely valid. Tenniel's pictures were popular and very much reflected the views of the middle classes. So even though this cartoon is Tenniel's interpretation, it represents broader opinion.

Definition

Fenian

This is nickname for a member of an organisation known as the Irish Republican Brotherhood, which was set up by James Stephens and John O' Mahony in 1858 to fight British rule in Ireland. A Fenian in the middle ages and before was an Irish warrior.

1.2 Map showing the main cities and counties in Ireland.

What was the Protestant Ascendancy?

The Protestant Ascendancy was the domination of Irish political and economic life by members of the Church of Ireland. The Church of Ireland was the official or Established church and the sister church of the Church of England. In the sixteenth and seventeenth centuries, large tracts of land in Ireland were taken by the government from the Catholic landowners and peasantry and were given to Protestant settlers from Britain. The motivation for such reallocation of land was to secure British rule and Protestantism in Ireland:

- Most of these Protestants were members of the Church of Ireland.
- Other settlers, primarily from Scotland, were **Presbyterians** who settled mainly in the northern Irish province of Ulster.

The defeat of the forces of the Catholic king James II in 1691 by the Protestant King William III at the Battle of the Boyne was a crucial turning point. From this moment onwards Catholics and, to a lesser extent, Presbyterians were discriminated against by a series of Penal Laws:

- The main aim of the Penal Laws was to force Catholics to convert to the Church of Ireland. Throughout most of the eighteenth century, Catholics were not allowed to vote, sit in Parliament in Dublin (or Westminster), join the legal profession or even own a horse over the value of £5. The Penal Laws were relaxed for Catholics in the 1790s and Catholics who owned property freehold worth 40 shillings or more were given the vote. But many Catholics still argued for the end of all discrimination and full emancipation.
- Presbyterians and other non-conformists were also discriminated against but to a lesser degree. Indeed the laws against Presbyterians were relaxed far earlier than those against Catholics, for example, from 1707 Presbyterians were allowed to sit as MPs although they were not allowed to hold public office.

The power of the Protestant Ascendancy lay in its control and ownership of the land; by the end of the eighteenth century, 95 per cent of the land was owned by members of the Church of Ireland. The topic of land is one that we will keep coming back to. Up until 1801, Ireland had its own Parliament which met in Dublin. Because of the fact that the Penal Laws discriminated against Catholics and Presbyterians, Parliament was dominated by the Protestant Ascendancy.

Rebellion and union

In 1798, a group of Irish people, known as the United Irishmen and led by Wolfe Tone, attempted a rebellion against British rule in Ireland. The rebellion was crushed by the British and 30,000 people lost their lives including Tone, who committed suicide. The uprising of 1798 was one of a series of examples of revolutionary nationalism in Ireland; the use of revolution and violence as a means of getting the British out of Ireland.

Definition

Presbyterians

These are Protestants whose church was run in a different way to the Churches of England or Ireland. They did not recognise the British monarch as their head, nor did they believe in bishops. Because they, and other Protestant groups such as the Quakers, did not conform to the rules of the established Church of England and Ireland, they were called non-conformists.

The answer to the 1798 uprising from the British Prime Minister, William Pitt the Younger, was to push for an Act of Union between Britain and Ireland. Such an Act would shut down the parliament in Dublin, amalgamating it with the one at Westminster. Pitt's proposal was opposed by many Protestant landowners in Ireland who believed that union would weaken the Ascendancy; the Dublin Parliament had represented their interests. But the government was determined and, on 1 August 1800, the Union Bill received royal assent. Under the Act of Union:

- 100 MPs representing Irish constituencies were to sit in the House of Commons at Westminster and Irish peers were given seats in the House of Lords.

- The Churches of Ireland and England were united into one Church.

- Ireland's trade was to be brought into line with Britain's in a customs union.

Despite his political triumph in getting the Act of Union through Parliament, Pitt failed to persuade King George III to agree to the clause in the Bill that proposed to give Catholics Emancipation.

What was the campaign for Catholic Emancipation?

The fact that Pitt failed to secure Emancipation for Catholics shows how strong the opposition to such a move was. It was not just the king who disliked Catholicism, there was a deep seated suspicion in Britain of Catholics and Catholicism that sprung from the sixteenth and seventeenth centuries. Below are the views of a famous Scottish philosopher and writer, David Hume, whose *History of England* (originally called the *History of Britain*) was published in six volumes between 1754 and 1762. Hume's work was widely read and was considered to be the standard history of England until Thomas Babington Macaulay's *History of England*, which was written in the following century. Indeed, Hume's work was so popular that it went through thirty-six editions. It is fairly likely, therefore, that Hume's attitude towards the Catholic Irish was probably shared by many in Britain.

Definition

Catholic Emancipation

This would involve giving Catholics the same rights of representation and civil liberties as enjoyed by Protestants.

Source B

The Irish from the beginning of time had been buried in the most profound barbarism and ignorance. They were sunk below the reach of curiosity and love of ideas which every other people in Europe have experienced. Their ancient superstitions mixed with wild opinions still have an unshakable hold over them. The example of the English following the Reformation did not alter the prejudices of the discontented Irish. So their old opposition to manners, laws and interests was made worse by religious antipathy. The subduing and civilising of Ireland was made more difficult.

From David Hume's *History of England* published in 1754

Question

What are the main points made by Hume in this extract?

But the forces in favour of Catholic Emancipation in Ireland were stronger than those, such as Hume, who would deny their freedom. A growing Catholic middle class in prosperous towns such as Waterford demanded change. Many Irishmen, who had fought for Britain in the Napoleonic Wars against France and under the leadership of the Irish Protestant Duke of Wellington, demanded Emancipation as a right.

Biography

Daniel O'Connell (1775–1847)

Daniel O'Connell was born in Cahirciveen, County Kerry, in 1775. Trained as a lawyer, he became well known for arguing that peaceful means should be used to obtain political and religious equality for Catholics. In 1823 he set up the Catholic Association which campaigned for Emancipation and Repeal of the Union. Even though the former was achieved in 1829, O'Connell continued to campaign for reform in Ireland. In 1843 he promised that he would achieve Repeal of the Union but was unsuccessful. In the last few years of his life, O'Connell came under criticism from nationalists who believed that his tactics were ineffective. Daniel O'Connell died in Genoa in 1847.

1.3 Daniel O'Connell

Definitions

Papist

is another word used to describe a Catholic (usually disparaging).

Catholic Association

Initially set up by O'Connell as a middle-class based organisation in 1823, the Association was turned into a mass movement by the introduction of the 'Catholic Rent', the contribution to the Association of a penny a month. Money raised was used to help fund election campaigns for Association candidates as well as supporting Association members who had been evicted from their homes. The Association forged very strong links with the Catholic Church, which collected the Catholic Rent.

Source C

Oh Wellington, sure you know it is true,
In blood we were drenched at famous Waterloo,
We fought for our king to uphold his crown,
*Our only reward was – **Papists** lie down*

From A. Jackson's *Irish Ballad* published in 1820

Catholic Emancipation was primarily won as a result of the campaigning of Daniel O'Connell and the **Catholic Association**, set up in 1823. The Association's agitation and campaigning reached a peak in 1828 in a by-election in County Clare. O'Connell, a Catholic, won the election but could not take his seat because of the discriminatory Penal Laws. A critical point had been reached because O'Connell and the Catholic Association had succeeded in mobilising popular support. Without a change in the government's stance on Emancipation, Ireland threatened to slide into revolt, or at best would be ungovernable. The writing was on the wall for the Penal Laws as even the Prime Minister, the Duke of Wellington (who had always been a staunch opponent of Catholic Emancipation), realised.

Source D

We have a rebellion impending over us in Ireland . . . and we have in England a Parliament, the majority of which is of the opinion, with many wise and able men, that the remedy is to be found in Roman Catholic emancipation.

From A. Jackson *The Duke of Wellington* published in 1828

Emancipation was a very important turning point in the relationship between Britain and Ireland. It showed that change could take place through constitutional means; O'Connell used elections as his greatest weapon to put pressure on the government. It also showed that the threat of rebellion could and did accompany legitimate demands for reform. It was in the campaign for Catholic Emancipation that constitutional nationalism was born. It was to come to prominence again later in the century in the campaign for repeal of the Act of Union and later in favour of Irish Home Rule. As a result of Emancipation, O'Connell was able to take his seat as a Member of Parliament at Westminster.

Why did O'Connell want repeal of the Union?

O'Connell did not rest after the victory of achieving Catholic Emancipation. While Emancipation was a political victory, it did not gain for Ireland the self-government and the destruction of the Protestant Ascendancy that O'Connell so despised. So, throughout the 1830s and much of the 1840s, O'Connell campaigned for the repeal of the Act of Union and a creation of a Catholic-dominated Parliament in Dublin. Yet O'Connell did not want to cut ties with Britain (see Source E) and he was loyal to the British monarchy, especially Queen Victoria, who came to the throne in 1837. Indeed in 1839 O'Connell made a loyal address of gratitude to the new queen. O'Connell spoke Irish but did not argue in favour of the restoration of the Irish language. His nationalism is very well summarised in the following speech made in the House of Commons in 1834. O'Connell is introducing a motion to repeal the Union between Britain and Ireland.

Source E

I would not . . . fling British connection to the wind. I desire to retain it. I am sure that separation [between Britain and Ireland] will not happen in my time; but I am equally sure that the connection cannot continue if you maintain the Union on its present basis. What then do I propose? That there should be that friendly connection between the two countries which existed before the Union. What I look for is that friendly connection by which both countries would be able to protect each other. As Ireland exported corn to England, so could England export her manufactures to Ireland – both countries would afford mutual advantage to the other. We have our viceroy [the monarch's representative] and our Irish peers; we only want a House of Commons which you could place on the same basis as your **Reformed Parliament** . . . In the name of Ireland, I call on you to do my country justice. I call on you to restore her national independence.

From D. Hepburn 'Daniel O'Connell's speech to the House of Commons', made on 22 April 1834

Question

What is O'Connell's arguing in this speech and how far does he want to divorce Ireland from Britain?

Definition

Reformed Parliament

In 1832 the Great Reform Act had changed the composition of Parliament by giving the vote to the middle classes. It also removed some of the more corrupt aspects of the previous electoral system, such as rotten boroughs, which were constituencies with hardly any voters.

Definition

Sedition

This is a charge laid against those people whose words or deeds are said to undermine monarch or state.

It is worth noting that O'Connell's proposal won little support in the House of Commons. Indeed the vote on his motion was 523 votes against with only 38 votes in favour. However, the cause he put forward was popular in Ireland, as was he. The campaign for repeal took off in July 1840 with the creation of the Loyal National Repeal Association. By the summer of 1843, the campaign for Repeal had peaked. 'Monster' meetings took place across Ireland in favour of O'Connell's call for the end to the Union. The largest meeting at Tara, County Meath, on 15 August 1843 was said to have attracted a crowd as large as three quarters of a million people. The climax of the campaign was to be a meeting at Clontarf on 8 October 1843. The authorities feared violence and banned the meeting. O'Connell, being a constitutional nationalist, did not object. In 1844, O'Connell was imprisoned for **sedition**. In the end he was found not guilty of the charges laid and, on his release, he made a triumphal procession through Dublin.

Source F

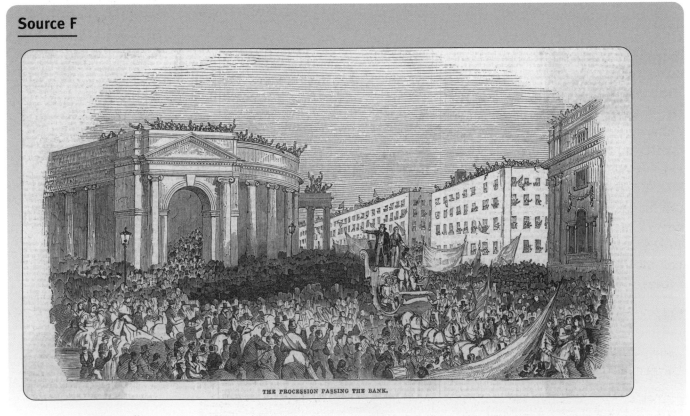

THE PROCESSION PASSING THE BANK.

1.4 Daniel O'Connell's acquittal, Dublin 1844.

How did Unionism develop?

O'Connell's aim for Repeal was an ideal. He did not take into account the bitter opposition to Repeal amongst the Presbyterian Protestants of the north of Ireland. In 1801, many of those who had rejected Union with Britain were Protestants who wished to keep a Parliament in Dublin to protect the Protestant Ascendancy. O'Connell's campaigns for Emancipation and Repeal changed all of that. Slowly but surely, the cause of the Union became a Protestant one as Presbyterians and members of the Church of Ireland increasingly saw the position of the Protestant minority in Ireland being best protected by union with Britain. There were to be, in the coming decades, individual Protestants who argued for a nationalist solution, most noticeably Charles Stewart Parnell. However, the Protestant working man increasingly identified with the unionist cause. The most significant organisation to represent their views was the **Orange Order**, which was founded in 1795 to protect the Protestant cause. By the 1820s the Order had a membership of around 100,000 Protestants. There were other clubs and societies that sprung up in the 1820s to defend Protestantism, including anti-Catholic **Brunswick Clubs**. By 1828 there were 200 such clubs in Ireland. Occasionally the government acted to curb the Protestant societies and clubs for fear that they were secretive organisations: the Orange Order was banned from 1836 to 1845.

Who was Henry Cooke?

The leader of the Protestant cause was the Presbyterian and Evangelist Henry Cooke. Throughout the late seventeenth and eighteenth century, the Presbyterians had identified more with the Whig political tradition. At the heart of the **Whig** tradition was an acceptance of **non-conformism**. However, in response to the campaigning of O'Connell and Tory, then Conservative, sympathies with the Protestant cause, Presbyterian sentiment slowly but surely aligned with Conservatism. Cooke argued that all Protestants, Presbyterian or Church of Ireland, should act as one to defend the common cause. In 1832 the Whig party took power. One of their first actions was an attempt to reform the Church of Ireland through the Irish Church Temporalities Act. This strengthened the common cause between Tories who opposed such reform and Irish Protestants.

Cooke identified his conservatism in the following terms:

Source G

To protect no abuse that can be proved, to resist reckless innovation, not rational reform; to sacrifice no honest integrity to hungry clamour; to yield no principle to time-serving expediency; to stand by religion against every form of infidelity.

From a speech made by Henry Cooke in Belfast on 22 January 1841

In January 1841, O'Connell visited Belfast to promote the cause of repeal. He was given a hostile reception. Cooke spoke to a huge crowd on 22 January of that year.

Definitions

Orange Order

The Order was named after King William III of Orange who had successfully defeated the Catholic forces of James II at the Battle of the Boyne in 1689, thereby ensuring the Protestant Ascendancy.

Brunswick Clubs

Formed in the heat of the debate about Catholic Emancipation in 1827–8, the Brunswick Clubs stood firmly against any concession to the Catholics.

Whig

The Whigs were the political grouping in Britain which stood for the power of Parliament and limited powers of the Crown. Their opponents were the Tories who stood for maintaining the established political order.

Non-conformism

was belonging to a church other than the established Church of Ireland.

Question

Study Sources F and G. What are the main points of Cooke's political philosophy?

Behold the great ideas of Protestantism and liberty, sitting inseparable in their power, while the genius of industry . . . reclines at their feet. Yes, Mr O'Connell, we will guard our liberties, and advance and secure the prosperity of our country. Look at the town of Belfast. When I was myself a youth I remember it almost a village. But what a glorious sight does it now present – the masted grove within our harbour – our mighty warehouses teeming with the wealth of every climate – our giant manufactories lifting themselves on every side. And all this we owe to the Union . . . Mr. O'Connell . . . Look at Belfast, and be a Repealer – if you can.

From a speech made by Henry Cooke in Belfast on 22 January 1841

What was the extent of agrarian violence?

While O'Connell and Cooke traded speeches about the desire for Repeal, others in Ireland took more direct means to deal with what were, for many, more pressing issues. In 1830 farmer agitation in the south-east and midlands of Ireland against paying the tithe erupted into violence. The so-called 'Tithe War' is a useful case study of how the government in London often responded to problems in Ireland. The Tithe was a tax to be paid to the Church of Ireland, irrespective of the religion of the payer. In the late 1820s and 1830s, opposition to payment spread. Secret societies were formed, known as 'Whiteboys', who raided farms, attacked animals and livestock and threatened the landlord. London's response was to strengthen the powers of the police; from 1826 to 1830, eighty-four people were killed in clashes with police. The violence continued to escalate; in June 1831 at Newtownbarry, County Wexford, twelve tithe demonstrators were shot dead, the same year that eleven police officers and soldiers were killed by an ambush of protesters. The response of the government was partly coercion: the Peace Preservation Act of 1833 laid down harsh penalties for offenders. The government also tried conciliation, including the Tithe Rent Charge Act of 1838, which removed many of the tithes. This dual approach of coercion and conciliation was to be much practised by the British government over the years.

RESEARCH TOPIC

Peel's Reforms

From 1841 to 1846, Conservative Prime Minister Robert Peel introduced a series of reforms to deal with some of Ireland's issues. It is your task to research some or all of the following:

- Charitable Requests Act 1844
- Maynooth Grant 1845
- Repeal of the Corn Laws 1846.

Who were Young Ireland?

Young Ireland emerged, in part, to support O'Connell's campaign for Repeal. Through the pages of the hugely popular *The Nation*, founded in 1842, the leaders of Young Ireland, including Thomas Davis, John Blake Dillon and William Smith O'Brien, argued for Irish cultural unity, education and complete separation from Britain. Even though they accepted some of Prime Minister Robert Peel's reforms to conciliate Ireland, they inspired future revolutionary nationalists with an ideal of an entirely free Republic. They increasingly quarrelled with O'Connell to the point that, in July 1846, they split from the Repeal movement. One of the arguments was over the use of violence, something that O'Connell opposed. In response to O'Connell's arguments, a 23-year-old member of Young Ireland, Thomas Francis Meagher, made a speech that eventually became known as the Sword Speech.

Source I

For, my Lord, I do not abhor the use of arms in the vindication of national rights. There are times when arms will alone suffice, and when political improvement call for a drop of blood, and many thousand drops of blood. The man that will listen to reason – let him be reasoned with, but it is the weaponed arm of the patriot that can alone prevail against battalioned despotism. Be it for the defence, or be it for the assertion of a nation's liberty, I look upon the sword as a sacred weapon.

Thomas Francis Meagher, 28 July 1846

Source J

Poor old Dan. Wonderful, mighty, jovial and mean old man, with silver tongue, smile of treachery, heart of unfathomable fraud.

From John Mitchel 'The New York Citizen' published by *Jail Journal* in 1854. He is writing about Daniel O'Connell.

The bitterness of the relationship between the 'constitutional' O'Connell and the increasingly 'revolutionary' Young Ireland can be seen in leading Young Irelander John Mitchel's attack on Daniel O'Connell in 1854. The *Jail Journal*, in which the attack first appears, was published in Mitchel's American paper 'The New York Citizen'. The *Jail Journal* was full of Mitchel's reflections on his transportation, his colleagues, Young Ireland and the 1848 Young Ireland movement.

Encouraged by revolution in France in 1848, Young Ireland leader William Smith O'Brien led an armed revolt which ended in the Battle of Widow MacCormack's cabbage patch. The response of the British government was to deport Smith O'Brien and the other leaders of the uprising to Tasmania. The uprising was a failure but the debate about Ireland and its future was to be overshadowed by a terrible tragedy.

What was the Great Famine?

One of the most famous British writers of the early part of the nineteenth century was Thomas Carlyle. His historical work *The French Revolution* published in 1837 was highly acclaimed and became a bestseller. However,

Carlyle was clearly extreme in some of his attitudes, and even criticised the abolition of slavery. In 1839 he expressed his views about the Irish. How mainstream his views were is debatable.

Discussion point

What is your reaction to Carlyle's views? What do his views tells us about the attitudes of the time?

> **Source K**
>
> Crowds of miserable Irish darken all our towns. Their wild features salute you on all highways and byways . . . The Irish is the sorest evil this country has to strive with. In his rags and laughing savagely, the Irishman is there to undertake all work that can be done by mere strength of hand and back, for wages that will buy him potatoes. The Englishman too may be ignorant, but he has not sunk from decadent manhood to squalid apehood.
>
> England is guilty towards Ireland and reaps at last in full measure the fruit of fifteen generations of wrong-doing. . . . The time has come when the Irish population must either be improved a little or else exterminated.
>
> From Thomas Carlyle's *Chartism* published in 1839

What caused the Famine?

The tragedy is that, just a few years after Carlyle's comments, a considerable proportion of the Irish population faced famine and death. The roots of the Famine lay in an over-reliance on the potato as the sole source of food. It also lay in the regions of Ireland, especially in the west of the country, where there was no industry and the farming was based on subsistence. In 1845 the *Phytophthora infestans*, a fungus that attacked the potato, struck. The Irish potato crop was all but destroyed in the ground as it was the following year of 1846 and in 1848. The result was, between 1845 and 1851, the deaths of around a million Irish people due to starvation and disease with perhaps one and a half million Irish people emigrating around the world.

What were reactions to the Famine?

Those who were hungry and had the energy tried to take matters into their own hands. Here is a scene from a food riot in Dungarvan on 10 October 1846, as represented by the *Pictorial Times*. The *Pictorial Times* was first published in London in 1843 as a rival to the highly successful *Illustrated London News*. Its aim was to report the news using pictures and very well written text. There is no suggestion that the pictures in the *Pictorial Times* misrepresented what happened, although there is a possibility that they were sensationalised. Have a look at this picture and see what you think.

Source L

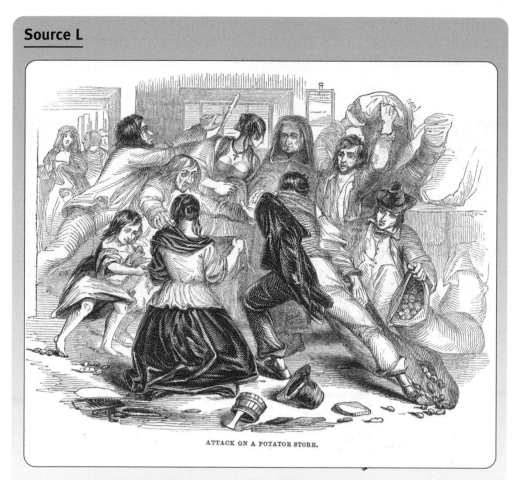

ATTACK ON A POTATOE STORE.

1.5 Galway in 1842, published in the *London Illustrated News*.

SKILLS BUILDER

Study Source L.

What does this picture show?

To what extent do you think that the picture gives an accurate interpretation of events in Dungarvan? Explain your answer fully.

Many in Britain were sympathetic towards the Irish; the Queen gave money to voluntary relief schemes as did thousands of others. However, as we will see, the government's view was not so generous, being bound up in the economic theory and political philosophy of the period. Some shared Carlyle's attitude towards the Irish and showed little sympathy. Source M is an extract from *The Times* newspaper from 1846.

Source M

The [Irish] people have made up their minds to report the worst and believe the worst. Human agency is now denounced as instrumental in adding to the calamity [disaster] inflicted by Heaven. It is no longer submission to Providence, but a murmur [complaint] against the Government . . . The Government provided work for a people who love it or not. It made this the absolute condition of relief. The Government was required to ward off starvation, not to pamper indolence [laziness]. Alas! the Irish peasant has tasted of famine and found it was good . . . There are ingredients in the Irish character which must be modified and corrected before either individuals or Government can hope to raise the general conditions of the people . . . For our own part, we regard the potato blight a blessing. When the Irish cease to eat just potatoes they must become meat eaters. With the taste of meat will grow an appetite to eat more meat; with this appetite comes a readiness to earn the money to pay for the meat.

The Times newspaper editorial, 22 September 1846

Source N

Being aware that I should have to witness scenes of frightful hunger, I provided myself with as much bread as five men could carry, and on reaching the spot I was surprised to find the wretched hamlet apparently deserted. I entered some of the hovels to ascertain the cause, and the scenes which presented themselves were such as no tongue or pen can convey the slightest idea of. In the first, six famished and ghastly skeletons, to all appearances dead, were huddled in a corner on some filthy straw, their sole covering what seemed a ragged horsecloth, their wretched legs hanging about, naked above the knees. I approached with horror, and found by a low moaning they were alive – they were in fever, four children, a woman and what had once been a man. It is impossible to go through the detail. Suffice it to say, that in a few minutes I was surrounded by at least 200 such phantoms, such frightful spectres as no words can describe, either from famine or from fever. Their demoniac yells are still ringing in my ears, and their horrible images are fixed upon my brain.

On 24 December 1846, *The Times* newspaper in London printed a letter from a Cork magistrate Mr Nicholas Cummins describing a visit to Skibbereen in County Cork

SKILLS BUILDER

Sources M and N are from the same newspaper. How can the historian explain such significant differences in opinion?

What did the government do about it?

Despite widespread hunger and starvation, the government's response was inadequate. The government of Robert Peel in 1845 and 1846 encouraged the creation of local relief committees and imported grain from Canada for sale. They also provided work, and therefore the means to pay for food, through public work programmes. The workhouses of the **Poor Law** were overrun. The government of Lord John Russell, which followed in the summer of 1846, gave Treasury Assistant Secretary Charles Trevelyan responsibility for deadline with the crisis. By 1847 the crisis was too great for the government to handle; there were 750,000 Irish people employed on the public works programme by the spring of 1847. However, Trevelyan and Russell's government were driven by *laissez faire* (see page 15) ideology and works programmes were scrapped in 1847 to be replaced by soup kitchens. As winter approached in 1847, the soup kitchens simply could not cope with the demand for food. Many landlords showed great kindness towards their tenants but others evicted those who were starving and penniless. The anguish caused by the Famine led some in Ireland to point the finger of blame at the British government. Here is an extract from a book by Young Ireland leader John Mitchel. In the extract Mitchel is writing about the Famine:

Source O

I have called it an artificial famine: that is to say, it was a famine which desolated a rich and fertile island that produced every year abundance and superabundance to sustain all her people and many more. The English, indeed, call the famine a 'dispensation of Providence'; and ascribe it entirely to the blight on potatoes. But potatoes failed in like manner all over Europe; yet there was no famine save in Ireland. The British account of the matter, then, is first, a fraud – second, a blasphemy. The Almighty, indeed, sent the potato blight, but the English created the famine.

John Mitchel writing in *The Last Conquest of Ireland (Perhaps)* published in 1861

The British did not create the Famine. The reaction of the British government was often slow and British ministers and civil servants were too tied to economic and political theory. However, the view of Mitchel and other stuck in the minds of many Irish people. The Famine showed the limitations of both the Irish land system and of British rule. Its main impact was to tie these two issues together at the forefront of British politics for the next fifty years.

Unit summary

What have you learned in this unit?

The history of Ireland in the first half of the nineteenth century was complex. You have learned about the main issues that dominated the relationship between Britain and Ireland: the Union, Catholic Emancipation, agrarian violence, Young Ireland and the Great Famine. You are now set up to look at Ireland from the middle of the nineteenth century onwards.

What skills have you used in this unit?

You have evaluated a range of different sorts of source material. You have also compared, cross-referenced and drawn inferences from them. You have also discussed contemporary values that come out of Sources A–O as a means of helping to understand the issues of the day.

Definitions

The Poor Law

The Poor Law was the means of helping the poor in Britain and Ireland. Relief was given inside a workhouse or through what was called 'outdoor relief', that is, allowances given to supplement the wages of the poor living in the community. Money to look after the poor was raised via the poor rate, a local tax on those with a certain amount of wealth. In 1834, the Poor Law was amended to make it harder for the poor to claim outdoor relief. Instead they were encouraged to seek relief in a workhouse based on the principle of less eligibility; that the conditions inside the workhouse would be worse than those outside. The Poor Law system was inadequate to deal with the scale of the problems faced in 1846.

Laissez faire

This was the dominant political and economic philosophy of most of the first half of the nineteenth century. It revolved around the belief that the government should interfere as little as possible, thereby allowing the natural laws of economics to function.

SKILLS BUILDER

1 Work in groups. Each of you must choose a theme:

   (i)   Constitutional nationalism (see Introduction, pages v–vii);

   (ii) Revolutionary nationalism (Source H, page 10);

   (iii) Unionism (Source K, page 12).

   Each of you should define the theme and give examples of how it manifested itself in the first half of the century.

2 There were clearly a number of issues that informed the relationship between Britain and Ireland: union, repeal, emancipation, religion, land and famine.

Your task is to put these issues in order of importance in defining the relationship between Britain and Ireland in the period 1798 to 1867. You should explain each issue and then why it is more or less significant than the others.

Exam style questions

This is the sort of question you will find appearing on the examination papers as an (a) question:

1 Study Sources E, H and K.

   How far do Sources E and H support the view of the relationship between Britain and Ireland explained in Source K?

Exam tips

- **Don't** bring in a lot of your own knowledge. All (a) questions focus on the analysis, cross-referencing and evaluation of source material. Your own knowledge won't be credited by the examiner, and you will waste valuable time writing it out.
- **Do** remember that the only own knowledge you should introduce will be to put the sources into context. This means, for example, that you might explain that Source E is a speech in Parliament, or that Thomas Carlyle was deeply prejudiced.
- **Don't** describe (or even re-write) the sources: the examiner will have a copy of the exam paper!
- **Do** draw inferences from the sources concerning what they show about the relationship between Britain and Ireland, and cross-reference the inferences for similarity and difference.
- **Do** reach a supported judgement about 'how far' Sources E and H support Source K by carefully weighing the similarities and differences.

Now try this question. Remember that this one is not asking about support, but about challenge. The approach, however, should be the same and you should use the exam tips in the same way.

2 Study Sources M, N and O.

To what extent does Source O challenge the interpretation of the Famine in Sources M and N?

RESEARCH TOPIC

The Famine

This introductory unit has touched on the Great Famine as a highly significant turning point in Ireland's history. You are to undertake research in depth about the Famine. Here are some questions that you might wish to answer:

- What was the extent of the Famine?

- How uniform across Ireland was the impact of the Famine?

- Why did the emigrants go?

- What were the main consequences of the Famine?

need to do.

2 Land, 1848–91

What is this unit about?

This unit focuses on the most important issue to dominate the relationship between Britain and Ireland in the second half of the nineteenth century: the land. It will look at the distribution of land and the challenges to the land holding system. In this unit you will find out about:

- the demands for change in the landholding system;
- the changes that took place through legislation.

Key questions

- Why was there such unrest in Ireland over the issue of land from the 1850s to the 1890s?
- How effective were organisations such as the Land League and their tactics of rural violence in bringing about change?

Timeline

1848–1850	Cholera epidemics
1851	Census: the population of Ireland has fallen to 6,552,000
1870	Gladstone's Land Act gives tenant farmers the right to compensation if they have made improvements to the land
1879	The Irish National Land League is formed. It demands the 'three Fs', fair rent, fixity of tenure and free sale of land
1880	Boycott: a new verb enters the language 'to boycott'. Charles Stewart Parnell, the leader of the Land League declares that if a tenant is evicted and somebody else takes over the land, that person is to be ostracised. The first person so treated was a Captain Boycott
1881	The Land Act grants the 'three Fs'. The Land Commission is formed to fix rent and to give loans to purchase land
1885	The Ashbourne Act allows for loans to be given to tenant farmers to buy their land. The loans are to be repaid at low rates of interest
1891	Purchase of Land (Ireland) Act makes more money available to tenant farmers to buy land

What was the post Famine crisis?

The Famine was an unprecedented disaster for rural Ireland, especially in the west of the country. Many of those peasants who survived the Famine hardship faced further difficulties. Most Irish peasants were tenant farmers, which meant that they rented their property and land from landowners. Most landlords owned about 2,000 acres but a few were very much better off; in 1870, 302 landowners (1.5 per cent of the total number of landowners in Ireland) owned a third of the land in the country. Around 25 per cent of landlords did not even live in the country. The Famine made matters worse for landlord and tenant. Here is a selection of contemporary and secondary sources to help you identify some the major issues in Ireland. Source A is from the *London Illustrated Times*, which had first been sold on the streets of London in 1842. In its first edition, the editorial had promised that it would not take sides in party politics.

Source A

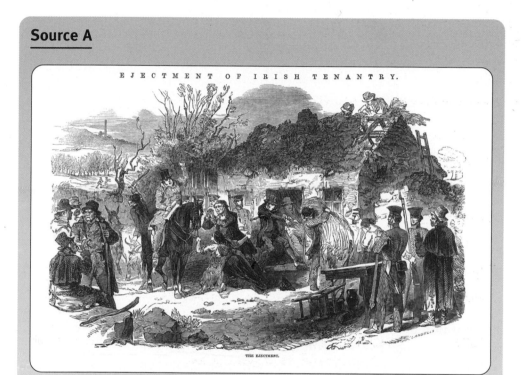

2.1 Irish tenants being evicted from their homes. Taken from the *London Illustrated Times*, 16 December 1848.

SKILLS BUILDER

Look at the drawings below and explain where you think that the sympathies of the artist lie:

1 How are the peasant, the landlord and the bailiff represented?

2 What images are there in the picture to evoke sympathy?

After reading through Sources B–J answer the following question:

How far do you think that these pictures have been exaggerated?

Source B

The failure of the potato crop brought economic pressure on Irish landlords who were confronted with both diminishing rentals and with the immediate burden of the poor law; many were quick to transfer this pressure to their tenants, either through severe measures to collect the rent or through eviction.

From A. Jackson *Ireland 1798–1998* published in 1999

Source C

The terrible clearances of the late 1840s were not sustained throughout the period: of the 90,000 evictions apparently recorded from 1847 to 1880, 50,000 took place between 1847 and 1850.

From R.F. Foster *Modern Ireland 1600–1972* published in 1988

Source D

Outside Ulster there was no compensation for improvement to a [tenant's] holding. This was both a barrier to agricultural development and a very great source of injustice, for there was no incentive to improve a property and those few tenants who ventured their capital in a holding had, in the event of an eviction, no right of redress.

From A. Jackson *Ireland 1798–1998* published in 1999

Source E

Most farmers, however, did not have a lease of their farms. Instead they were tenants-at-will, which meant that they could be legally evicted whenever the landlord chose. Another complaint against landlords was that they spent very little money on improving the farms.

From E.G. Power *Modern Ireland* published in 1988

Question

From studying Sources B–E above, what can you identify as the problems facing Irish agriculture in the wake of the Famine?

Question

What are Lalor's proposed solutions to the Irish land question?

What were the solutions?

The position of many tenant farmers in Ireland at the end of the 1840s was dire. The popular image of an uncaring landlord class had become common currency. The reality of the situation was more complex, as we shall see later in this unit. However, the Famine and its aftermath led many to believe that the two issues of the future of the nation and the land question were closely related. They therefore presented solutions which were both radical and different. The best known and most relevant commentary came from James Fintan Lalor.

James Fintan Lalor was from a wealthy landowning family. He was also a member of Young Ireland. Lalor came to the conclusion that the Famine was the fault of the landowning class to which, ironically, he himself belonged. He took part in the uprising of 1848 and wrote for the Young Ireland newspaper *The Nation*. He also wrote letters to and for the nationalist newspaper *The Irish Felon*, which was set up in June 1848. While his ideas were considered too extreme for the time, they were to have a big influence on the nationalist movement of the future and its leaders, including Michael Davitt, James Connolly and Arthur Griffith. The following letter from Lalor was published in *The Irish Felon* on 24 June 1848. The extract is a lengthy one but it is important that you read it through.

Source F

It is a mere question between a people and a class – between a people of eight million [the Irish] and a class of eight thousand [the landlords]. They or we must quit this island. It is a people to be saved or lost – it is the island to be kept or surrendered. They have served us with a general writ of ejectment . . . They do not now, and never did belong to this island. Tyrants and traitors have they ever been to us and ours since first they set foot on our soil. Their crime it is and not England's that Ireland stands where she does to-day – or rather it is our own that have borne them so long.

I hold and maintain that the entire soil of a country belongs of right to the people of that country, and it is the rightful property not of any one class, but of the nation at large, in full effective possession, to let to whom they will on whatever tenures, terms, rents, services, and conditions that they will; one condition, however, being unavoidable, and essential, the condition that the tenant shall bear full, true, and undivided fealty, and allegiance to the nation, and the laws of the nation whose lands he holds, and own no allegiance whatsoever to any other prince, power, or people, or any obligation of obedience or respect to their will, order or laws.

The land question contains, and the legislative question does not contain, the materials from which victory is manufactured; and that, therefore, if we be truly in earnest and determined on success, it is on the former question, and not on the latter that we must take our stand, fling out our banner, and hurl down to England our gauge of battle.

From James Fintan Lalor's letter to *The Irish Felon*, 24 June 1848

SKILLS BUILDER

Lalor's views were considered radical for the time. Explain the context in which his letter has been written and published. In your explanation you might consider the following:

- The aims of Young Ireland.
- The situation in Ireland in 1848.

What were the 'three Fs'?

One more moderate way ahead encouraged by Lalor and others was the formation of tenant organisations devoted to securing tenants' rights. In August 1850, an Irish Tenant League was founded by Charles Gavan Duffy. Its aim was to improve the position of tenant farmers in Ireland whatever their denominational background. The League itself did not last long; by 1852 it had become the Independent Irish Party. However, it brought to the fore the campaign for the 'three Fs': free sale, fair rent and fixity of tenure. What did these actually mean?

- *Free sale* meant selling the 'interest' in a holding to the next tenant. Already practised in Ulster (and known as the 'Ulster Custom') free sale also involved the tenant being compensated for improvements made to the holding. Free sale was practised outside Ulster but unevenly so.
- *Fair rent* in reality meant a low rent and one fixed by a tribunal rather than by the landlord. The popular image was of greedy landlords engaged in 'rackrenting', that is, the setting of very high rents. The reality, as we will see, was more complex.
- *Fixity of tenure* was guaranteed tenure of land over a period of time.

Case study: What was the reality of the state of Irish agriculture between 1850 and 1879?

Here is an example of the more traditional explanation of the problems of Irish agriculture in the period.

Discussion point

Why might this interpretation be considered simplistic?

Source G

The sufferings of the Irish were in considerable measure due to the prevalent system of land tenure. There was a vast difference between the rural landlord in England and his Irish counterpart – the former putting money into the land and making improvements for the tenants; the latter merely drawing rack-rent, leaving the tenants to do everything for themselves, and often evicting them wholesale without compensation for improvements.

From the *Encyclopaedia of World History* published in 1952

Below are two more updated interpretations, both by highly respected historians, and a chart. You are to use sources to explain the reality of Irish agriculture between 1850 and 1879.

Source H

Generally, they [the landlords] continued to make profits, rather than investment, the priority . . . The 'typical' landlord owned about 2,000 acres; but by 1876 less than 800 landlords owned half the country:

- 302 (1.5 per cent of the total) owned 33.7 per cent of Irish land;
- 13.3 per cent owning 23 per cent of the land, were resident outside the country.

The picture of landlords as 'vampires' (Davitt) has long been disproved; if post-Famine Irish landlords were vampires, they were not very good at it. Certainly, income was stressed above investment . . . but J. Donnelly's survey of Cork finds landlords putting more money in after 1850 [into] new stock, drainage techniques and experiments.

How did they treat their tenants? Farms were generally held on yearly arrangements; but the law considered these leases as practically renewable. As to actual rent levels, it is very difficult to generalise. On a subsistence-level holding in Connemara, any rent was too high; while on a large farm in the Midlands, rent fell far behind price levels. Rent increases between the Famine and the Land War ran at a low rate.

Adapted from R.F. Foster *Modern Ireland 1600–1972* published 1988

Source I

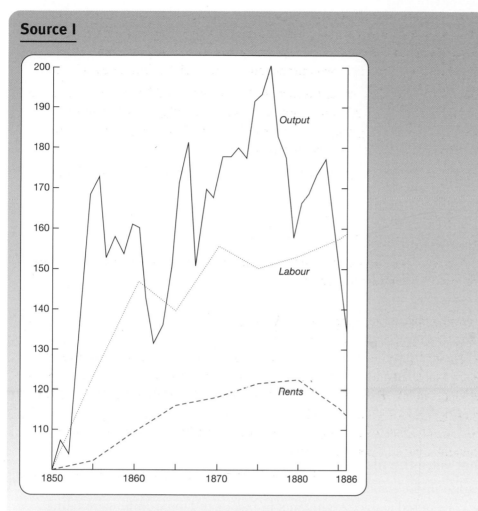

2.2 Agricultural output, rents and labour costs 1850–86.

From W.E. Vaughan, 'Landlords and Tenants in Ireland in 1848–1904', *Studies in Irish Economic and Social History*, No 2

Source J

The stereotype of the predatory, cruel landlord applies only to a handful of bullies such as the Earl of Leitrim. The old stereotype has been replaced by that of the benign [kind] proprietor who, though hardly in the vanguard of change himself, gave progressive tenants a fair field . . . Far from being inevitable or prompted by landlord wrongs, the Land War followed almost three decades of tenurial peace and growing prosperity . . .

In reality, post-Famine landlords rarely resorted to eviction, and when they did it was nearly always for non-payment of rent . . . Rent rose less than agricultural prices, and rent levels were such that . . . the average tenant could ride out even the worst years. Landowners now gave more value for their money, paying more attention to the day-to-day running of their estates and to agricultural improvement than did their fathers.

From Cormac Ó Gráda *Ireland: A New Economic History, 1780–1939* published in 1994

Definition

Home Rule

As we will see later on in this book (see pages 54–81), the idea of Home Rule is deceptively complex. However, in simplest terms, it involved the devolution of some powers to an Irish Assembly in which decisions would be made about Irish affairs.

Biography

William Gladstone (1809–98)

Born in 1809, Gladstone was one of Britain's greatest Prime Ministers. He served as Prime Minister four times: from 1868 to 1874, 1880 to 1885, 1886 and 1892 to 1894. Originally a disciple of Conservative Prime Minister Robert Peel, he became a Liberal in 1859. Gladstone's liberalism revolved around the promotion of individual liberty. Gladstone devoted much energy to Ireland, including the attempts in his third and fourth ministries to introduce **Home Rule**.

What were the reasons for the 1870 Land Act?

Despite improvement in conditions through the 1860s, the situation was not considered stable. Arguments in favour of Home Rule were being proposed by Irish politicians such as Isaac Butt (who we will look at in greater depth in Unit 3). Violence lay not far below the surface of Irish political life. In 1870 the first of a series of laws was passed to rectify some of the grievances of Ireland's tenant farmers. The Prime Minister in 1870 was the Liberal leader William Gladstone. These are some of the reasons why he decided to introduce the Land Act.

Fenianism

The emergence of Fenianism will be explained in far greater detail in the next unit (see pages 37–59). However, it is worth briefly outlining at this point who the Fenians were and their impact on British politics and leaders, including Gladstone. Fenianism emerged in the 1850s out of Young Ireland, the large-scale emigration to America (which again will be explained in more detail in Unit 3) and mid-nineteenth century revolutionary nationalism. The Irish Republican Brotherhood and its American counterpart, the Fenian Brotherhood (both founded in 1858), were committed to change through insurrection. In 1867 a Fenian Uprising led to the execution of three of its members: William Allen, Michael Larkin and William O'Brien. The result was martyrdom, which was to have important consequences. Those who believed in constitutional means for resolving Ireland's problems had greater sympathy for Fenianism. As a result, more Fenians were prepared to collaborate with the more constitutionally minded, especially when addressing issues of land and Home Rule. It was to prove to be a heady alliance. It was also something that Gladstone noticed.

Tenant Right

An economic downturn in the late 1860s saw the revival in 1869 of the Irish Tenant League led by Sir John Gray. The League's agenda was based on the addressing of the 'three Fs' and the momentum for the movement was provided by a great Land Conference held in February 1870. At the Conference, proposals were agreed upon for the best way ahead.

Gladstone

Gladstone's political thinking and agenda for land reform in Ireland was influenced by the conservative National Association set up by Cardinal Cullen in 1864. Above all else, Gladstone aimed to improve the situation of Ireland's tenant farmers. His determination to reform can be seen in the speech below to an election rally in 1868.

Source K

The Fenian conspiracy has been an important influence with respect to Irish policy.

William Gladstone speaking in the House of Commons on 31 May 1869

Source L

The Church of Ireland . . . is but one of a group of questions. There is the Church of Ireland, there is the land of Ireland, there is the education of Ireland; there are many subjects, all of which depend on one greater that all of them; they are all so many branches from one trunk, and that trunk is the tree of what is called the Protestant Ascendancy. We therefore, aim at the destruction of that system of ascendancy.

William Gladstone speaking in an election meeting in Lancashire in 1868

Questions

1 What were Gladstone's priorities with regards to Ireland?
2 Why was Gladstone prepared to undermine some of the main features of the landholding system that had supported the Protestant Ascendancy.

When Gladstone heard in 1868 that he was to become Prime Minister, he declared, 'My Mission is to Pacify Ireland'. His First Ministry was marked by a number of attempts to tackle Irish issues through reform. These will be explained in Unit 3 (see pages 37–59). The centrepiece of his reform programme was the Irish Land Act of 1870. However, he and his Cabinet faced a number of obstacles. It was simply not politically possible to introduce radical reform to the landholding system in Ireland; such a move would be very unpopular with Members of Parliament and peers in the House of Lords. Gladstone decided, therefore, that the best course of action would be to legalise custom.

What were the terms of the Land Act 1870?

The main points of the Act attempted to address some aspects of the 'three Fs':

- The tenant who was evicted for reasons other than non-payment of rent had the right to compensation for any improvements made.

- By the so-called 'Bright Clauses' of the Act, government loans (5 per cent interest repayable over 35 years) could be made available to tenants who wished to buy their holdings from their landlords. The tenants were allowed to borrow from the government up to two-thirds of the cost of buying their holding. There was no compulsion on the landlord to sell.
- Rents were not to be 'exorbitant' (the original Bill which was changed by the House of Lords had included the word 'excessive').

However:

- The Act failed to create a tribunal system for the regulation of rent and it failed to prevent the possibility of unfair rent increases.
- Tenants with leases longer than thirty-one years were not protected by the Act.
- Some landlords responded by changing the length and nature of their tenants' leases to place them outside the Act.
- Fewer than 1,000 farmers took advantage of the 'Bright Clause', most being unable to afford to borrow such money.
- Tenants still lacked protection against eviction.
- Rural violence continued and the government's response, even as the Bill was passing through Parliament, was to introduce the Peace Preservation Act 1870, which increased its powers of repression. In 1871 the Westmeath Act gave police forces powers to arrest those suspected of being members of secret societies.

On the other hand:

- The Act was symbolically very important indeed; it set a precedent for government intervention in the land question.
- By stating that the tenant had the right to compensation, Gladstone had accepted that the tenants had an interest in their holdings, albeit a moral one.

Question

To what extent does the 1870 Land Act mark a significant breakthrough for Irish land reform?

Biography

Michael Davitt (1846–1906)

Michael Davitt was born in 1846 in County Mayo, Ireland. On being evicted from their home, his family moved to Lancashire in 1852 where they found work in the cotton mills but in 1857 Michael lost his right arm in a factory accident. Davitt's interest in radical Irish politics led him to join the Irish Republican Brotherhood (IRB) in 1865 and in 1867 he was involved in a raid on Chester Castle. Davitt was imprisoned in Dartmoor in 1870 after being convicted of gun running. While imprisoned, he came to the conclusion that the solution to the land question was the redistribution of land and the best means was non-violence. Poor agricultural conditions led Davitt to set up the Land League of Mayo in 1879 from which sprung the National Land League. In 1882 Davitt was elected as an MP for County Meath. From this point until his death in 1906 he campaigned tirelessly for the causes of justice and reform through peaceful campaigning. He was one of the founder members of the British Labour Party and his methods of protests were an inspiration to many, including Mahatma Gandhi.

How did the Land War start?

Despite the strengths of the agricultural system and the impact of Gladstone's reforms, there were still periodic crises in the countryside. Indeed there had been an economic crisis between 1859 and 1864, the like of which had not been seen since the 1840s and the Great Famine.

Crisis hit the countryside again in the late 1870s. Poor harvests were recorded in 1877 and 1878. Cheap imports of food from America into Britain meant that prices of agricultural goods dropped across Ireland; in Cork and Tipperary the price of butter fell by as much as 60 per cent. Perhaps most worryingly, in the west of Ireland, potato production fell by up to 75 per cent. Money from migrants, which usually supported the poor, had dried up as Britain also fell into temporary recession. On 20 April 1879, a huge crowd met in Irishtown, Country Mayo to call for reduced rents and protest against the actions of Catholic priest and landlord Canon Ulick Burke, who had threatened to evict his tenants. The following account was written by Michael Davitt in 1904. One should, therefore, treat his account with a certain degree of caution.

Source M

[The country] has not been in so critical a condition since the year 1847. Three successive bad harvests have reduced farmers – particularly the smaller class – to a very low ebb. The country shopkeepers, who are dependent on the farming and labouring population, cannot collect the money due to them.

An Ulster Bank circular published in 1863

Source N

The Dublin press did not report the demonstration nor even allude to it in any way. It was not held under official home-rule auspices, while the fact that one of its objects was to denounce rack-renting on an estate owned by a Catholic clergyman would necessarily, at that early stage of a popular movement, frighten the timid editors of Dublin from offering it any recognition. But the local prestige won by the meeting was enormous. The speeches were fully given in the Connaught Telegraph. The meeting had within a few days knocked five shillings in the pound off the rentals of the estate which was singled out for attack. This news flew round the county, and requests for meetings reached the organisers from various districts.

From Michael Davitt *The Fall of Feudalism in London* published in 1904

SKILLS BUILDER

Given this source was written by Davitt and given what it says, how might you challenge the emphasis of the source and even what it says?

To answer this question you might comment on the following:

- the language of the source;
- the claims made in the source.

The immediate impact of Davitt's campaigning was that Canon Burke reduced his rent by 25 per cent. The wider and far greater significance of the Mayo campaign was that Davitt and Parnell used it to turn an economic downturn into a political crisis.

- In October 1879, the National Land League of Ireland was founded with Parnell as President. This was a crucial turning point. Parnell added to the already politically explosive issue of Home Rule a version of the radical agrarian agenda provided by Lalor.

- The campaign that followed turned the Home Rule and nationalist party into an **umbrella movement**.

- Parnell himself successfully walked a political tightrope; on the one hand, he encouraged the support of the revolutionary Fenians without ever supporting the idea of a nationalist revolution. On the other hand, Parnell supported the use of more extreme tactics in the countryside (see Source O) without ever approving Davitt's proposals that the land should be nationalised.

Definition

Umbrella movement
An umbrella movement is a movement that includes a number of viewpoints.

What were the tactics of the Land League?

The Land League was the perfect opportunity for Parnell and the other leaders to rally all elements of the nationalist movement. The issue of land reform drew support from all sections of Irish society, while the radical tactics of what today would be called 'direct action', drew the more revolutionary elements of the nationalist movement such as the Fenians into the wider nationalist movement. The aim of the Land League and the purpose of the Land War were to defend the tenant against the unregulated excess of the landlord. The following extract is from a speech given by Parnell in Country Clare, which was reported in *The Times* newspaper on 20 September 1880. Even though *The Times* was unsympathetic to the cause of the Land League, it is unlikely that it would have misquoted or misrepresented Parnell's words.

Question

What tactics is Parnell suggesting the peasantry should adopt and how radical were such actions?

Source O

Depend upon it that the measure of the Land Bill of next session will be the measure of your activity and energy this winter. It will be the measure of your determination not to bid for farms from which others have been evicted, and to sue the strong force of public opinion to deter any unjust men amongst yourselves, and there are many such, from bidding for such farms. If you refuse to pay unjust rents; if you refuse to take farms from which others have been evicted, the land question must be settled, and settled in a way that will be satisfying to you. Now, what are you to do to a tenant who bids for a farm from which another tenant has been evicted? . . . When a man takes a farm from which another has been evicted, you must shun him on the roadside when you meet him, you must shun him in the streets of the town, you must shun him in the shop, you must shun him on the fair-green and in the market place, and even in the place of worship, by leaving him alone, by putting him into a moral Coventry, by isolating him from the rest of his country, as if he were the leper of old, you must show him your detestation of the crime he has committed . . .

From Charles Stewart Parnell's speech reported in *The Times* newspaper on 20 September 1880

Source P

NO RENT!
NO LANDLORDS' GRASSLAND

Tenant Farmers, now is the time. Now is the hour.
You provide false to the first call made upon you
Redeem your character now.

NO RENT
UNTIL THE SUSPECTS ARE RELEASED

The man who pays Rent (whether an abatement is
offered or not) while Parnell, Dillon &c. are in Jail
will be looked upon as a Traitor to his Country
and a disgrace to his class.

No RENT, No Compromise, No Landlords'
Grassland, Under any circumstances.
Avoid the Police and listen not to spying and
debting Bailiffs.

NO RENT! LET THE LANDTHIEVES DO THEIR WORST!
THE LAND FOR THE PEOPLE!

2.3 A Land League poster, 1881.

SKILLS BUILDER

What are the similarities in the proposals of Source O and of
Source P?

The Land League used a range of methods in waging its war against the
landlords.

- Posters, campaign rallies and slogans went hand in hand with the
  implicit threat of violence.
- As suggested by Parnell, rents were withheld and farms where evictions
  had taken place were left empty.
- Those landlords who continued to evict were at best ignored and at
  worst were subjected to violence and even assassination.

- In September 1880, landlord Lord Mountmorres was murdered in what was a widely reported crime on both sides of the Irish Sea.

Case study

The case of Captain Boycott: The best known case of ostracisation from the community was that of Captain Boycott and his family. Indeed, the case became so well known that the word *boycott* subsequently entered the English language. Captain Boycott was an English landlord of an estate in County Mayo and agent on the estate of Lord Erne. In September 1880, Boycott served notices on eleven tenants on Lord Erne's estate who had failed to keep up with rent payments. In response, the local community (including the local priest Father John O'Malley) encouraged all of Boycott's servants and workers to leave his estate. Boycott's response was to write to *The Times* newspaper.

Source Q

People collect in crowds upon my farm and order off all my workmen. The shopkeepers have been warned to stop all supplies to my house. My farm is public property, I can get no workmen to do anything, and my ruin is openly avowed as the object of the Land League unless I throw up everything and leave the country.

By the editor of *The Times* newspaper in an editorial published on 18 October 1880

Source R

The persecution of the writer, Mr Boycott, for some offence against the Land League's code, is an insult to the government and to public justice.

From an anonymous writer of *The Times* newspaper editorial published on 18 October 1880

The story of Captain Boycott was a news sensation and it provoked considerable reaction.

The publicity led to fifty people from Ulster volunteering to help Captain Boycott. They were mainly Orangemen who wished to make a point. Arriving under troop escort in November 1880, they worked for two week to help bring Boycott's crop in before departing. Despite their crops being successfully harvested, the boycott of Captain Boycott and his family intensified rather than abated. Realising that they had no future in Ireland, Boycott and his family departed for England at the end of 1880. The boycott had succeeded.

The view of the Illustrated London News

The question to ask is how objective was the reporting of the Boycott case. Below are an artists impression and a written newspaper report that were both published in the *Illustrated London News*. Lough Mask House in County Mayo was the home of Captain Boycott.

Source S

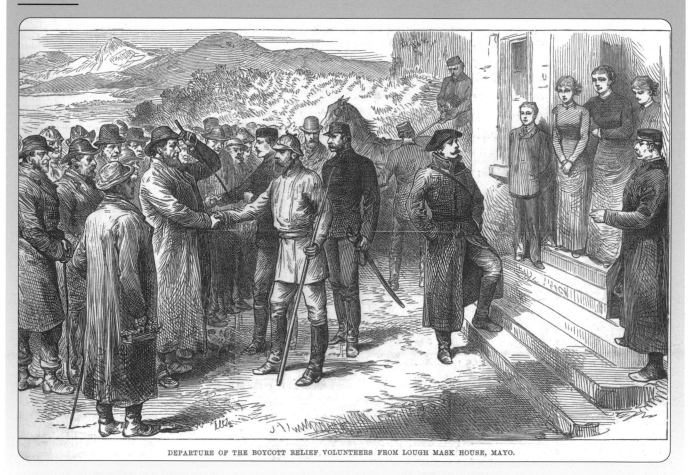

DEPARTURE OF THE BOYCOTT RELIEF VOLUNTEERS FROM LOUGH MASK HOUSE, MAYO.

2.4 Departure of the Boycott relief volunteers from Lough Mask House, Mayo, published in the *Illustrated London News* on 4 December 1880.

Source T

A band of fifty volunteers from the counties of Cavan, Fermanagh, and Monaghan, came to Lough Mask, as we have related to perform this work gratuitously [for free] for Captain Boycott. The government send a large military force to protect them, as well as to protect the gentleman and his family, and a regular encampment was formed in his grounds. The party of Ulstermen, mostly sons of farmers have borne many days of fatigue, worry, and exposure to bitter wintery weather, in an exemplary spirit. No attempt has been made to molest them; and the work of reaping and digging the various crops, and of threshing the corn has duly finished. On Saturday last, at two in the afternoon, the camp was broken up; and the Ulster party, taking leave of by Captain and Mrs. Boycott, marched to Ballinrobe.

From the *Illustrated London News* published on 4 December 1880

SKILLS BUILDER

What evidence is there in Sources S and T that suggests that the *London Illustrated News* was sympathetic to Captain Boycott and his family?

What were the main points of the 1881 Land Act?

Gladstone's response to the continuing agitation was the 1881 Land Act. The main aims of the Act were short-term and, to an extent political rather than economic, to reduce the level of unrest in the country by reducing rents. To that end the main points of the Act were:

- An Irish Land Commission was set up to decide levels of rent where there was a dispute.

- Tenants had the right of free sale of holdings.

- The concept of 'statutory tenure' was established; tenants were to have security of tenure as long as it was certain that they were abiding by certain conditions.

But all were not satisfied.

The Act placed Parnell in a difficult position. While it resolved the 'three Fs', at least superficially, it did not satisfy many of the more radical members of the Land League who wanted redistribution of land. So Parnell argued that the Act was inadequate and should be tested in the courts. In March 1881, Parliament passed a Coercion Act aimed at clamping down on unrest and those who encouraged it. Indeed, Parnell argued all too strongly in public for the liking of Gladstone or his Chief Secretary for Ireland, W.E. Forster, and he was thrown into Kilmainham Gaol in October 1881. From his cell, Parnell issued a 'No Rent Manifesto' that called for a national rent strike. In many senses, the 'No Rent Manifesto' was as much about trying to keep the broad coalition of the Land League together as it was a response to the 1881 Act. In Source U you can read an extract from the manifesto issued by Parnell.

Source U

Fellow-countrymen! – The hour to try your souls and to redeem your pledges has arrived. The executive of the National Land League, forced to abandon the policy of testing the Land Act, feels bound to advise the tenant-farmers of Ireland from this day forth to pay no rents under any circumstances to their landlords until the government relinquishes the existing system of terrorism and restores the constitutional rights of the people. Do not be daunted by the removal of your leaders. Your fathers abolished tithes by the same method without any leaders at all, and with scarcely a shadow of the magnificent organisation that covers every portion of Ireland today. Do not suffer yourselves to be intimidated by threats of military violence. It is as lawful to refuse to pay rents as it is to receive them. Against the passive resistance of an entire population military power has no weapons. Do not be persuaded into compromise of any sort by the dread of eviction. If you only act together in the spirit to which, within the last two years, you have countless times solemnly pledged your vows, they can no more evict a whole nation than they can imprison them. The funds of the National Land League will be poured out unstintedly for the support of all who may endure eviction in the course of the struggle.

From a 'No Rent' declaration signed by Charles Parnell in October 1881

Punch magazine presented a different viewpoint.

Source V

PUNCH, OR THE LONDON CHARIVARI.—August 13, 1881.

THE RIVALS.

2.5 *The Land Act is Handed to Hibernia*, published in *Punch* on 13 August 1881.

The Act did not take into account those tenants who were in arrears. By an agreement between Gladstone and Parnell made in May 1882 (and part of the condition for Parnell's release from prison) known as the 'Kilmainham Treaty', it was agreed that those tenants in arrears would effectively have the slate wiped clean. In the longer term the treaty did little for the health of Ireland's rural economy. Indeed, by fixing tenure and by lowering rents, the Act supported the *status quo*.

How did rural agitation develop in the 1880s and into the 1890s?

There was periodic unrest in the 1880s and early 1890s in Ireland, based on fluctuating economic conditions. Government was dominated by the Conservatives who were prepared to balance conciliation with coercion and 'kill' the land issue 'with kindness'.

SKILLS BUILDER

1 Explain the message of the cartoon. How does the characterisation compare to the other *Punch* cartoon studied so far (see Source A on page 2)?

2 How does Source V's reaction to the 1881 Land Act compare to that of Source U?

Ashbourne Purchase Act 1885

In June 1885, a Conservative ministry led by Lord Salisbury sought support from Irish nationalists in Parliament by passing what was an imaginative piece of legislation. The Act enhanced the policy of land purchase by providing a sum of £5 million for loans with which tenants could buy their holdings on a low interest long-term basis.

In 1886–87 the agricultural economy deteriorated again and the National League reconvened under the leadership of old land campaigners, including John Dillon and William O'Brien. In October 1886, they launched a 'Plan of Campaign'. The aim of the Plan was to force rents down through the use of collective action. The idea was relatively simple, in that all tenants would get together and agree the rent they wished to pay. If the landlord refused then the tenants would not pay their rent, those being evicted being supported by their fellow tenants and, ultimately, the League. In the end, the threat of a rent strike was only carried out on 203 estates and those were usually where the landlord was in debt and, therefore, was vunerable.

The response from the Conservative Government was the usual mix of coercion and conciliation. On the one hand, the Land Act of 1887 built on Gladstone's Land Act of 1881, by allowing leaseholders to participate in the rent arbitration scheme. On the other hand, the Chief Secretary for Ireland, Arthur Balfour, was more than happy to use force as a means of curtailing the actions of those behind the Plan. On 9 September 1887, the Royal Irish Constabulary opened fire on a demonstrating crowd in Mitchelstown, County Cork, killing three and wounding many more. However, Balfour strongly supported Land Purchase Acts passed in 1888 and 1891 which extended Ashbourne's Purchase Act of 1885; the 1888 Act provided a further £5 million for the scheme. By the 1890s, therefore, the emphasis had shifted.

Question

What are Cormac Ó Gráda's arguments regarding the Land War?

What was the impact of the land agitation?

Here is an interpretation of the outcome of the struggle for land in the 1870s and 1880s.

Source W

The gist of Barbara Solow's influential study of the Land War was that the protracted struggle that began in 1879 was unnecessary. [Another historian] W.E. Vaughan's assessment went further, considering its outbreak a fluke, and its outcome at least a draw from the tenants' standpoint. Further, it is claimed, landlord exploitation cannot explain the origins of the Land War, nor can it be proved that the tenants won the battles of 1880–82 or 1887–90. The struggles of the 1880s and 1890s, far from putting an end to evictions, only provoked many more of them, and failed to reduce rents significantly. Worst still, according to Solow, the Land War put an end to landlord investment and distracted farmers from the business of farming. While the Irish plotted and fought, the Danes and Dutch increased their hold on the British market for dairy and pork products.

From Cormac Ó Gráda *Ireland: A New Economic History, 1780–1939* published in 1994

Unit summary

What have you learned in this unit?

By the end of the nineteenth century, considerable progress had been made in the status of tenant farmers in Ireland. They could purchase their property and legally own the land which many felt morally as theirs. The government had used legislation to improve the situation of the tenant farmer in the face of bitter and substantial campaigning. The impact of the land struggle on the rural economy is debatable.

The campaign for land reform became closely intertwined with the cause for Home Rule and Irish separatism. The fortunes of politicians, most notably Charles Stewart Parnell and William Gladstone were linked to their association with the land question. It is the question of Ireland's relationship with Britain to which we turn next.

What skills have you used in this unit?

You have used the skill of interpretation in trying to understand the differing arguments presented. You have compared and contrasted interpretation and you have investigated sources to establish the extent of subjectivity. In this unit you have worked with source material to establish the main arguments for land reform and you have evaluated source material in the light of its attribution and your own knowledge.

SKILLS BUILDER

1 Go back to the situation explained in Sources A to E.

   To what extent had the position of tenant farmers in Ireland changed by 1891?

2 Look at Sources O and U.

   How useful are such pieces of evidence to the historian in explaining Parnell's role and tactics in the Land War?

3 Work in a group.

   How justified were the tactics of the Land League?

To answer this you will need to identify the different aspects of the Land League's tactics. You will then need to discuss how far each of these tactics were justified.

Exam style question

This is the sort of question you will find appearing on examination papers as a (b) question:

Use Sources Q and W and your own knowledge.

- **Do** be clear about the question focus – what is being claimed? In this case, what is being claimed is that the Land League had achieved its aims.
- **Analyse** the sources to establish points that support and points that challenge the view given in the question.
- **Develop** each point by reference to your own wider knowledge, using it to reinforce and/or challenge the points derived from the sources.
- **Combine** the points into arguments for and against the stated view.
- **Evaluate** the conflicting arguments.
- Present a **judgement** as to the validity of the stated view.

And above all, **plan** your answer.

Do you agree with the view that the Land League's was successful in achieving its aims?

Start now by using the exam tips to draw up a plan that would deliver an answer to this question. You might find that using a spider diagram would be the best way to do this.

RESEARCH TOPIC

Irish migration

This subject has been touched on in the first two units. It is an important context to the next few units.

- Where did the Irish migrate to and in what numbers?
- How did they settle in their new communities?
- What was the impact on Irish politics of this migration?

3 Ireland 1860–85: violence and pacification

What is this unit about?

The last unit focused primarily on the issue of land. This unit aims to place that focus into a broader context by looking at the impact that Fenianism and the growing campaign for Home Rule had on political life in Britain and Ireland. While legislation of successive governments in this period is important, the emphasis in this unit will be on constitutional and revolutionary nationalism. In it you will:

- find out how Irish politics had an ever growing influence on British party politics;
- assess the impact of individuals, including Isaac Butt and Charles Stewart Parnell.

Key questions

- How did Irish nationalism develop from the mid-1860s to 1885?
- What was the impact of the development of revolutionary and constitutional nationalism on successive British governments and unionism?

Timeline

1858	James Stephens sets up the Fenian Brotherhood and Irish Republican Brotherhood
1863	Fenian newspaper *Irish People* is founded
1865	*Irish People* is shut down, James Stephens arrested but escapes from Richmond Jail
1867	
February	Fenian uprising in Chester and Kerry
March	Fenian rising across Ireland
June	Clan na Gael founded in New York
November	Manchester martyrs executed
December	Clerkenwell explosion
1868	Amnesty campaign for Fenian prisoners
1869	Irish Church Act leads to disestablishment of the Church of Ireland
1870	Gladstone's first Land Act
1875	Charles Stewart Parnell elected MP for County Meath
1876	IRB withdraws support from Home Rule movement
1877	Parnell appointed President of the Home Rule Confederation of Great Britain
1879	Irish National League founded

1879–82	Land War
1880	Boycott of Captain Boycott
1881	Gladstone's second Land Act. Parnell imprisoned
1882	Kilmainham 'Treaty' and Parnell's release. Phoenix Park murders Irish National League formed
1884	Agreement between National League and Church over education Representation of the People Act
1885	General Election returns eighty-six supporters of Home Rule

What was Fenianism?

Below is an extract from a speech made by the founder of Fenianism, James Stephens, in St Louis, Illinois, in the United States of America on 24 October 1866. In the speech, Stephens appeals for support for the Fenian cause but also outlines the nature and tactics of Fenianism. Stephens was in the United States to raise money for arms to fund a rebellion in Ireland and to encourage a Fenian attack on British North America (nowadays known as Canada) from the United States.

SKILLS BUILDER

1 What are the main points made by Stephens in his speech?

2 Given what Stephens says and the circumstances of his speech, how reliable is Stephens's account of the strengths of Fenianism?

Source A

James Stephens delivered an address at St Louis on Monday evening. He said: 'At one time, if we could have had 3,000 or even 5,000 more rifles than we had in the City of Dublin last December, we would have struck for Irish Independence that night. Then we could have taken the city and all the barracks; and could have marched out of Dublin with an English army and garrison in our hands.

I may as well tell you, gentlemen, that I am the founder of the Fenian Brotherhood in America as of the movement in Ireland . . . In a single county in Ireland there are 25,000 sworn members. There it is a military power, held together as firmly as any on earth. Here [in America] it is a loose agglomeration. The organisation [in Ireland] is stronger today than ever before [but] in point of preparation we have made but little progress beyond that of twelve months ago. I am here to procure arms and war material for the people, for we are bound to take the field [of battle] before the 1st of January. Let no man have any doubt about this. I repeat, I shall be on Irish soil this year and raise the flag of Ireland in battle. As already stated, our success, to some extent, depends on you.'

From the *New York Times* published on 26 October 1866

Biography

Giuseppe Mazzini (1805–72)

Mazzini was one of the important figures of romantic nationalism in Europe. He developed the concept of a united Italy, which was to be democratic, republican and devoid of foreign control. Throughout the 1830s, Mazzini's supporters used revolution as the means to effect political change, culminating in the Roman Republic in 1848–49. In 1860, another hero of romantic nationalism, Giuseppe Garibaldi, invaded Sicily with one thousand volunteers inspired by Mazzini's encouragement of popular revolution. His actions were to have a profound impact on the establishment of a new Italian state in 1861.

At the heart of Fenianism was a belief in the creation of an Irish republic and the end of British rule in Ireland. As you will have read from Stephens' speech, the Fenians' strategy was centred on armed insurrection. Just as Wolfe Tone and the United Irishmen in 1798 had hoped for foreign support for their cause (in this case the French), so many Fenians believed that their greatest opportunity for a successful uprising would be when Britain was involved in a war against a foreign power. This was a conclusion come to by other nationalist groups across Europe. Those hoping for the liberation of the Italian peninsular from Austrian domination from Giuseppe Mazzini to Count Camillo Cavour understood that this would not be achieved without foreign support. The late 1850s saw increasing tension between Britain and France and Stephens hoped that this might provide an opportunity for the Fenians.

Although the ultimate aim of the Fenians was the creation of an Irish Republic, there was diversity of strategy if not aims. Some Fenians, including leaders John O'Leary and Charles Kickham, were prepared to collaborate with the more constitutionally minded Irish nationalists. Indeed, they were even prepared to accept the supremacy of the British Crown in a self-governing Ireland. This again was not unique to Ireland. In Italy, republicans Giuseppe Mazzini and Giuseppe Garibaldi were prepared to work with the forces of King Victor Emmanuel of Piedmont to remove Austria's influence from the Italian peninsular.

Case study

Irish in the Armed Forces Throughout the nineteenth century, there was a very strong tradition of Irishmen serving in the British armed forces. In 1861 it was estimated that there were 55,000 Irishmen serving in the army and navy, many of them having fought in the Crimean War with great distinction. The tradition of Irish people serving the Crown continued through the First and Second World Wars, even up to the present.

Definitions

Diaspora

Is the dispersal of a people around the world and away from their original homeland. The Irish diaspora saw the Irish move in large numbers to Britain and North America but also to Australia and New Zealand.

Clan na Gael

In English means 'family of the Gaels' (a Gael is someone who speaks Gaelic). It was set up in 1867 as a rival organisation to the Fenian Brotherhood, which it eventually replaced by the 1870s as the dominant voice of Fenianism in the United States of America. From the early 1870s, Clan na Gael was led by John Devoy.

Social deference

This is when people will show respect to others because of their class rather than because of who they actually are.

So who were the Fenians?

The Fenian movement was a diverse one, in part because of the **diaspora** of the Irish people in the wake of the Famine.

In the United States of America Fenianism was especially strong amongst the Irish communities. Large numbers of Irish people flooded into the United States, in the 1860s, at a rate of around 100,000 a year. The Fenian Brotherhood was one of a number of organisations, others including **Clan na Gael** founded in 1867, which represented radical nationalist opinion. Many Irish exiles signed up to fight in the American Civil War and, through so doing, gained extensive military experience. In 1865 a Fenian convention decided that time was ripe for an invasion of British-ruled British North America (as Stephens had hoped they would) and, in June 1866, a Fenian force led by Colonel John O'Neill did just that. Their hope was that by attacking British territory, they would put pressure on the British government to grant Ireland a Republic. They were defeated by a mixture of Canadian militia and British troops at the Battle of Ridgeway in 1866. Two further Fenian raids in 1870 and 1871 were also repulsed.

In Britain there was also a strong Fenian community in the wake of strong Irish emigration to British towns and cities in the wake of the Famine. Although, according to the 1861 census, the proportion of Irish-born living in Britain was statistically low at 3.5 per cent of the population, this figure hid the large number of people of Irish descent who had been born in Britain. The Irish communities tended to congregate; there were perhaps 178,000 Irish-born in the north-west of England in 1861, in mill towns such as Blackburn and the port of Liverpool. Such communities fed on a hatred of the country in which they lived and there were perhaps as many as 80,000 Fenians in Britain in 1865. Many Fenians living in Britain were, ironically, serving in the British armed forces; the need to earn a living taking priority over ideology.

In Ireland its members were mainly from the lower middle class and the movement's leadership was controlled by the classes it represented. Therefore, Fenianism lacked the **social deference**, which was the mark of other movements including the Home Rule movement. It is estimated that, by the mid-1860s, there were 54,000 Fenians in Ireland, most in employment covering a range of trades and jobs from artisans and shopkeepers to journalists. For many Fenians, revolution and the destruction of the power of the landowning classes was the means to social as well as national advancement.

Fenianism and the Catholic Church

The Fenians also hoped to make Irish nationalism **non-sectarian** and **non-clerical** (see page 41). They also believed that issues such as the resolution of the land question were secondary and should be dealt with once the primary aim of independence had been achieved. Many Fenians were attracted to the ritual, ceremony and secrecy of the organisation. It was these elements of the movement which brought the Fenians into conflict with the Catholic Church because many within the Church suspected that the Fenians were **Freemasons**. In 1861 the Fenian Brotherhood arranged for the body of Young Irelander Terence MacManus to be brought to Ireland for a grand funeral but Catholic Archbishop Paul Cullen refused to become involved. The following source was written by Fenian Charles Kickham and was published in the Fenian newspaper *Irish People*, which was founded in 1863.

Source B

Nothing would please us better than to keep clear of the vexed question of 'priests in politics'. But the question was forced upon us. We saw clearly that the people should be forced to distinguish between the priest as a minister of religion and the priest as a politician before they could be got to advance one step on the road to independence. The people for whom God created it must get this island into their own hands . . . Our only hope is revolution. But most of the bishops and many of the clergy are opposed to revolution . . . We have over and over declared it was our wish that the people should respect and be guided by their clergy in spiritual matters. But when priests turn the altars into a platform; when it is pronounced a 'mortal sin' to read the *Irish People*, when priests actually call upon the people to be informers, and openly threaten to set the police upon the track of men who are labouring in the cause for which our fathers so often bled – when in a word, bishops and priests are doing the work of the enemy, we believe it is our duty to tell the people that the priests may be bad politicians and worse Irishmen.

From Charles Kickham's article published in the *Irish People* on 16 September 1865

SKILLS BUILDER

How reliable is this source as evidence of that relationship between Church and Fenian movement in the mid-1850s? In considering this question you need to take into account the following:

- the content of the source;
- the context in which it is written;
- the situation of the author;
- his purpose in writing Source B;
- the nature of the evidence.

What tensions were there between the Fenian movement and the Catholic Church in the mid-1860s?

Definitions

Non-sectarian

A non-sectarian organisation is one which is open to people from different faiths or groups. In the context of Fenianism and Irish history generally, groups that are non-sectarian hope to appeal to Catholics and Protestants.

Non-clerical

A non-clerical group is one which is not influenced by the Catholic Church.

Freemasons

Freemasons are people who belong to a secret international organisation that promotes mutual help between members. Freemason meetings follow distinct ritual and their belief in a Supreme Being rather than the Christian God brought Freemasons into bitter conflict with the Catholic Church.

Definition

Habeas corpus

This is a basic human right, which demands that anyone who is arrested must be brought to court to prove that he or she has a case to answer, or be released.

1867: The turning point

The events of 1867 were to have a profound impact on the cause of Irish nationalism and British attitudes towards Ireland. The authorities were fully aware of Fenian activities through a highly efficient ring of informers. Stephens' speech in St Louis was widely reported. In September 1865, the offices of the *Irish People* in Dublin were raided and the newspaper was shut down. The leadership of the Fenian Movement were arrested, including Stephens, although he later escaped from Richmond Gaol. Such was the government's concern that **habeas corpus** was suspended in February 1866, which made it easier to round up suspects and then keep them in custody without trial. Driven on by American Civil War veterans keen for the fight and English radicals keen to advance a republican cause, the Fenians launched a series of uprisings in 1867. Uprisings in Chester (where the arsenal at Chester Castle was unsuccessfully stormed) and County Kerry in Ireland in February were easily thwarted. This was followed in March by dismal failure in Cork, Limerick and Dublin. The risings failed because of poor organisation, uneven quality of leadership and the fact that the British police had many informers within the Fenian Movement.

The priority for Lord Derby's government in London was to crack down on the Fenian movement in Ireland and Britain. A number of Fenian leaders were arrested including, in Manchester in September 1867, Colonel T.J. Kelly and Timothy Deasy. As these two Fenian leaders were brought to court the following week, a gang of thirty Fenians staged a daring rescue. In the process of attacking the prison van in which Kelly and Deasy were being transported, a police officer, Sergeant Brett, was killed. A number of Fenians were arrested and three, William Allen, Michael Larkin and William O'Brien, were executed after being found guilty of Sergeant Brett's murder.

The significance of this event and its aftermath should not be underestimated. The Dublin based *Freeman's Journal* was the most widely read nationalist newspaper in Ireland for most of the nineteenth century. In the light of the 1867 executions, it commented:

Source C

Had this clever and daring manoeuvre been accomplished in an Irish town or even the Irish metropolis [Dublin, Belfast or Cork], it would create little surprise; but the rescue of an 'Irish Rebel' from the hands of the police in one of the great centres of England is a strange if not alarming illustration of the extent of the organisation and the capacity of those who direct it.

From the *Freeman's Journal* published on 19 September 1867

Source D

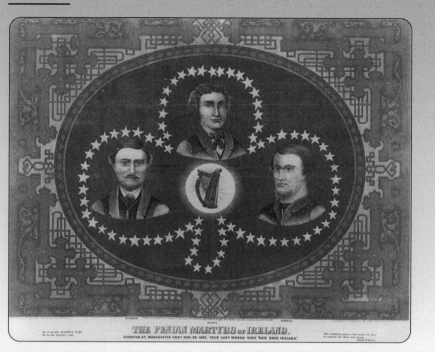

THE FENIAN MARTYRS OF IRELAND.

3.1 The 'Manchester Martyrs' poster produced in the United States of America, 1867.

British attitudes towards Fenianism

The executions of Allen, Larkin and O'Brien and their creation as 'martyrs' did much to reconcile many within the Catholic Church to Fenianism. Many in rural Ireland, who adhered to the Church line, were now far more accepting of Fenian aims and tactics. The so-called 'Manchester Martyrs' had shouted 'God Save Ireland' as they were led from the dock. This catchphrase symbolised the growing bond between Church and nationalism. The cause of Fenian and constitutional nationalist became blurred and many constitutionalists were drawn to the Brotherhood and many Fenians became part of the Land and Home Rule campaigns. In November 1869, Fenian prisoner Jeremiah O'Donovan Rossa was elected as MP for Tipperary.

There were distinct differences still between revolutionary and constitutional nationalists but these differences became blurred in the eyes of British public opinion. In December 1867, a group of Fenians attempted to rescue fellow Fenian from Clerkenwell **House of Correction** by blowing up a wall. The explosion was greater than anticipated and a number of innocent people lost their lives. There was public revulsion and anger directed against the Fenians and Irish people living in England. The German writer and philosopher Karl Marx, who was living in London at the time (and who might be expected to be sympathetic to the revolutionary aims of Fenianism), was horrified.

Discussion point

Using Sources C, D and your own information, what do you think was the impact of the execution of Allen, Larkin and O'Brien on the Fenian cause?

Definition

House of Correction

The House of Correction was where petty criminals would be put to hard labour in an attempt to reform their criminal ways. The aims of a House of Correction were to reform as well as punish.

SKILLS BUILDER

Why would the historian find Marx's comments useful? For advice on how to answer this question, go back to the Skills Builder on page 41.

Source E

This latest Fenian exploit in Clerkenwell is a great folly. The London masses, who have shown much sympathy for Ireland, will be enraged by it and driven into the arms of the government party. One cannot expect the London proletarians to let themselves be blown up for the benefit of Fenian emissaries. Secret, melodramatic conspiracies of this kind are, in general, more or less doomed to failure.

Letter from Karl Marx to Friedrich Engels on 14 December 1867

Case study: British attitudes in pictures

Source F

PUNCH, OR THE LONDON CHARIVARI.—December 28, 1867.

THE FENIAN GUY FAWKES.

3.2 'The Fenian Guy Fawkes' – sitting on a keg of gunpowder ready to explode. Illustration by John Tenniel published in *Punch*, 28 December 1867.

Source G

3.3 'The Irish Frankenstein' – anti-Irish cartoon depicting the Irish Fenian as a monster.

Engraving by Matt Morgan in *The Tomahawk*, 18 December 1869

Source H

3.4 'George and Fenian Dragon'. Cartoon depicting the Fenian dragon defeating Saint George.

Unattributed illustration in *The Tomahawk*, 1867

Source I

PUNCH, OR THE LONDON CHARIVARI.—DECEMBER 31, 1881.

TIME'S WAXWORKS.

(1881 *JUST ADDED TO THE COLLECTION.*)

Mr. P. "HA! YOU'LL HAVE TO PUT HIM INTO THE CHAMBER OF HORRORS!"

3.5 'Time's Waxworks' by John Tenniel published in *Punch*, 31 December 1881. Father Time introduces Mr *Punch* to the Fenian; the latest addition to the waxwork collection of Imperial problems.

Definition

Frankenstein's monster

As you will see at more than one point in this book, Fenianism and the Irish in general were depicted as Frankenstein's monster. A favourite of Victorians, it refers to the creature at the heart of Mary Shelley's Gothic novel. The great majority of those people studying the cartoons would recognise the character and understand the inference.

About the sources

We have already seen an example of John Tenniel's depiction of Irish people in the *Punch* cartoon on page 2. Two of the four sources above are also the work of John Tenniel. They both tell us much about attitudes towards the Irish as well as wider racial attitudes. *The Tomahawk* was a satirical magazine, which was published weekly between 1867 and 1870. It was the same type of publication as *Punch* and may well have appealed to the same readership. It was published for an educated, mainly London based audience and its pictures would have most likely reinforced rather than challenged their attitudes. On the other hand, *The Tomahawk* was known for its forthright views on Ireland; in the debate on the 1870 Coercion Act in Parliament it was mentioned that: 'A paper with such cartoons published in London, going over to Ireland and circulating there, would be far more mischievous than if originally printed in Dublin.'

SKILLS BUILDER

Study all four cartoons closely and answer the following questions. Your answers may be written down or may form part of a wider discussion.

1 What similarities are there between the sources in how the Irish are represented and why do such similarities exist?

2 What do these cartoons tell the historian about public attitudes towards Fenianism?

Home Rule and Isaac Butt

Isaac Butt emerged as a national leader in 1869 as President of the United Amnesty Association, which had been set up to campaign for the release of Fenian prisoners.

The significance of the Association was that it drew together different strands of nationalist opinion. In this sense the Association was the forerunner of the Home Government Association founded by Butt in May 1870 with the approval of many leading Fenians. Butt's views were clearly expressed in the following source:

Question

What are the main features of Home Rule as proposed by Isaac Butt?

Source J

I intend to propose a system under which England, Scotland and Ireland, united as they are under one sovereign, should have a common executive and a common national council for all purposes necessary to constitute them, to other nations, as one state while each one of them should have their own domestic parliament for its internal affairs.

The federal arrangement which I contemplate is one which would preserve the Imperial Parliament [at Westminster] in its present form. It would leave it still the power of providing by Imperial taxation for Imperial necessities.

The Irish Parliament consisting, be it always remembered, of the Queen, Lords and Commons of Ireland, would have supreme control in Ireland, except in those matters which the federal Constitution might specifically reserve to the Imperial Assembly [Parliament]. That which is important is that Ireland would send, as we do now, 105 representatives to vote in an Imperial Parliament on all questions on Imperial concern, and in return we would submit to be taxed, as we do now, to be taxed, but only for certain definite purposes.

At home in Ireland we would have our own Parliament controlling all of the affairs of our internal administration.

From Isaac Butt *Home Government for Ireland* written in 1870

Gladstone's reforms

In Unit 2 of this book, we read about Gladstone's claim on taking office that his 'mission was' to 'pacify Ireland'. It is well worth us having another look at his election speech made in Lancashire in 1868.

Source K

The Church of Ireland . . . is but one of a group of questions. There is the Church of Ireland, there is the land of Ireland, there is the education of Ireland; there are many subjects, all of which depend on one greater than all of them; they are all so many branches from one trunk, and that trunk is the tree of what is called the Protestant Ascendancy . . . We therefore, aim at the destruction of that system of ascendancy.

William Gladstone speaking in an election meeting in Lancashire in 1868

Now let us see how much of this he managed to achieve in his first ministry.

Issue 1 Disestablishment: The Irish Church Act 1869

At the heart of the Irish Church Bill was the proposal to **disestablish** the Church of Ireland. The Bill met with fierce resistance from Conservatives in the House of Commons and from the House of Lords generally. However, the Liberal majority of around 120 MPs ensured that the Bill passed through the House of Commons and, on the Queen's prompting, the Lords reluctantly passed it through their House. The Act stipulated the following:

- The Church of Ireland was to become a voluntary body but provision was make to made to look after the clergy.
- The Tithe payment was ended and Catholics were no longer obliged to financially support the Church of Ireland.
- The Church's assets were taken away, the Church receiving compensation of £10 million.

Issue 2 Land: The Land Act 1870

This has been explained in more detail on pages 18–36. However, to refresh your memory, the main points of the Act were:

- Evicted tenants were to be compensated for improvements made to the property while tenants.
- Government loans were made available to tenants who wished to buy their holdings from their landlords but landlords were under no compulsion to sell.
- Rents were not to be 'exorbitant'.

Biography

Isaac Butt (1813–1879)

Born in 1813, the son of a Donegal rector, Butt was perhaps the leading individual associated with law-abiding constitutional nationalism. Butt trained as a lawyer but, while initially unionist and conservative in his politics, he acted as defence lawyer for Young Irelanders in 1848 and numerous Fenians between 1865 and 1868. Butt did not wish to see the end of the Union but Home Rule within a federation. His achievement was to win the support of a number of Fenians and other revolutionary nationalists for the Home Rule cause. He died in 1879.

Definition

Disestablishment

An established Church is when it is the official Church of a state and receives support from the state. Disestablishment is when the status of a Church as the official Church of a state is removed.

Issue 3 Education: The Irish University Bill 1873

The failure of this Bill reflected the limitations of Gladstone's Ireland strategy. His proposals were to:

- Create a **secular** university in Dublin by combining Trinity College Dublin, Queen's College and a Catholic college.

- The new university would not offer potentially controversial subjects of history, philosophy or religion.

Despite Gladstone's large majority, the Bill was defeated by three votes in the House of Commons. The idea of attacking religious-based education was too much for many in Gladstone's Liberal Party as well as the Conservatives on the opposition bench.

How did the cause of Home Rule develop in the 1870s?

In 1873 Butt's Home Rule Association became the Home Rule League. The change was more than symbolic as the political movement had become a political party. Still with the support of many from within the Fenian movement, as well as a number of Catholic bishops, the cause of Home Rule was now one with considerable electoral support. The passage of the 1872 Secret Ballot Act was also to help the Home Rule cause; no longer would tenants be forced to vote in front of their landlords. In the General Election of 1874, around sixty of the MPs elected declared themselves to be in favour of Home Rule, over half of Ireland's MPs. Despite such an apparently sensational success for the Home Rule cause, Butt's campaign made little progress over the coming years.

- Although around sixty MPs were committed to the cause of a Federal system as proposed by Butt, many were Liberals first rather than Home Rulers.

- Butt was not effective in Parliament, in part because the Conservative majority was so large and because the Prime Minister Benjamin Disraeli was determined to avoid reform in Ireland.

- A more radical wing of the party emerged who were frustrated with Butt's leadership and the clear unwillingness of the Conservatives to introduce any meaningful reform. Some MPs such as Joseph Biggar obstructed business in the House of Commons by talking for as long as they could. Their aim was to talk until the time allotted for a piece of proposed legislation had run out. This was called 'obstructionism' and it made it difficult for any government to conduct the normal business of the House of Commons.

- The Fenian movement temporarily withdrew its support for Home Rule in September 1876. The pressure for such a move came from the American based Clan na Gael movement led by John Devoy. Although American based Fenians were prepared to support attempts at constitutional change, their support was not open-ended. By the mid-1870s, Devoy and others believed that Butt's approach had failed.

Definition

Secular

Secular means is the opposite of clerical. A secular university is one that is not based on religion.

Discussion point

This is a central issue and one worth discussing in groups.

How successful and how far reaching were Gladstone's Irish reforms from 1869 to 1873?

- In 1875 Charles Stewart Parnell was elected MP for County Meath. Parnell was prepared to shock Parliament by using the language of confrontation; a tactic that embarrassed Butt. In 1876 the Chief Secretary of Ireland, Sir Michael Hicks Beech, claimed in the House of Commons and referring to the 1867 Manchester incident that the Fenians were the 'Manchester Murderers'. Parnell's response was clear and significant:

Discussion point

Why do you think that Parnell made such a comment?

New departure

The 1870s were a watershed in Irish politics. The emergence of Parnell as leader of the Home Rule party and movement was quick in coming. In 1877 Parnell became President of the Home Rule Confederation. Parnell's political skill was in his ability to appeal to different strands of Irish nationalism. He was, by instincts, a constitutionalist who was prepared to work within the confines of legal means and Parliament. However, above all else, Parnell was an opportunist. He was prepared to weave together the different strands of Irish nationalism, thereby creating a force far more potent than if the threads of Buttite constitutional nationalism, Fenianism or land reform were left on their own.

Source L

I wish to say as publicly and directly as I can that I do not believe and never shall believe, that any murder was committed at Manchester.

Charles Stewart Parnell addressing the House of Commons, *Hansard*, 30 June 1876

Definition

Hansard

Hansard is the published record of what is said in Parliament. From 1829 to 1909, *Hansard* was in private hands but became an ever more reliable record as the nineteenth century progressed. From 1907, *Hansard* was produced by Parliament as the official record of proceedings.

Biography

Charles Stewart Parnell (1846–91)

To summarise the life or significance of Parnell in a few lines is a near impossible task. Born in 1846 into an Anglo-Protestant family, Parnell studied at Cambridge University and entered Parliament in 1875. After a brief period of settling in, he became the dominant Irish political figure until his death in 1891. His political achievements were many; he forced Home Rule and Land Reform to the top of the political agenda, in part by harnessing the more extreme nationalist elements. Parnell was a supreme political opportunist but his opportunism in his private life was to be his downfall. For many years he conducted an affair with Kitty O'Shea, wife of colleague William O'Shea. When the scandal broke, his party split and his career was finished. He died in Brighton in 1891.

Parnell's radical language and seeming embrace of aspects of the Fenian cause appealed to the leadership of the Fenian movement on both sides of the Atlantic. The leader of the Fenian Clan na Gael, John Devoy, telegrammed Parnell in October 1878 with the following proposal in what became known as the New Departure telegram.

Source M

Nationalists here will support you on the following conditions:

First: Abandonment of the Federal demand and substitution of a general declaration in favour of self-government.

Second: Vigorous agitation of the Land Question on the basis of a peasant proprietary, while accepting concessions tending to abolish arbitrary evictions.

Third: Exclusion of all sectarian issues from the platform.

Fourth: Irish members to vote together on all Imperial and Home Rule questions adopt an aggressive policy and energetically resist coercive legislation.

Fifth: Advocacy of all struggling nationalities in the British Empire and elsewhere.

Telegram from John Devoy to Charles Stewart Parnell, 25 October 1878

SKILLS BUILDER

1 What are the grounds for a compromise position between the Fenians and Parnell?

2 How does Devoy indirectly and directly criticise the conservative nationalism of Isaac Butt?

Liberal response

Although the 1874 to 1880 government of Benjamin Disraeli introduced little reform, they did, in response to pressure from Irish nationalists, introduce a University Education (Ireland) Act in 1879. The main provision of the Act was to create a new university, the Royal University, that would cater for Catholics and Protestants. The 1880 General Election was fought mainly on issues other than Ireland. However, that did not stop the Conservative leader Disraeli standing on an explicitly anti-Irish platform.

The 1880 election was a triumph for Gladstone although the Home Rule vote held up well, with up to sixty-three MPs committed to the Home Rule cause.

In fact, the terms of what became known as the 'New Departure' were not those outlined in Source M. The leadership of the Irish Republican Brotherhood (IRB) objected to its moderate tone. In 1879 a more radical

'New Departure' was proposed that was to bring together the aspirations of Michael Davitt, John Devoy and Charles Stewart Parnell. The scene was set for the Land War of 1879 to 1882, which was covered in Unit 2 of this book (see pages 27–36).

As you have seen on pages 48–49, the reaction of Gladstone's government to the agitation in Ireland was a dual approach of coercion and reform. Because of his refusal to support the main features of the 1881 Land Act and because of the negative impact of his party's tactics of challenging the Act, Parnell was imprisoned in Kilmainham Gaol in October 1881. In the same month the Land League was repressed by the government. Although imprisonment was not to Parnell's liking, it provided him with political opportunity. Imprisonment in a British jail meant that he could be portrayed as a martyr for the radical cause while in reality distancing himself from the violence. Once it became clear to members of the government, including Joseph Chamberlain, that the imprisonment of Parnell and other Land League leaders was not going to end the agitation in Ireland, they put out peace feelers. Parnell agreed to negotiate through a go between, Captain W.H. O'Shea (who happened to the husband of Parnell's mistress Kitty), with the British government. The resultant agreement, the so-called Kilmainham Treaty, saw Parnell released in April 1882. For its part, Gladstone's government agreed to look again at certain aspects of the Land Act that had disappointed the Land League; for his part Parnell agreed to co-operate with the Liberals on a reform programme for Ireland and he backed the amended Land Act.

What were the Phoenix Park Murders?

On 6 May 1882, the Chief Secretary for Ireland Lord Frederick Cavendish and Under-Secretary for Ireland, T.H. Burke were assassinated in Phoenix Park in Dublin by members of a previously unheard-of splinter group from the IRB known as the Invincibles. The murders caused revulsion in Ireland and Britain and were to have a significant impact on the course of Irish politics. The government was determined to clamp down on terrorism; for one thing, Lord Cavendish had been married to Gladstone's niece. Parnell was shocked by the murders and considered resigning from politics; in the end he did not do so but continued with his moderate line as signalled by the Kilmainham Treaty. The government introduced draconian measures, including the Prevention of Crimes Act 1882, which suspended trial by jury and allowed the police power to search and arrest people on suspicion.

Despite his condemnation of the murder of Cavendish and Burke, sections of the media were quick to link Parnell to the assassinations, an assertion that was to be made in 1882 and later on in the decade. Below is an example of the type of reaction at the time in the popular press:

Source N

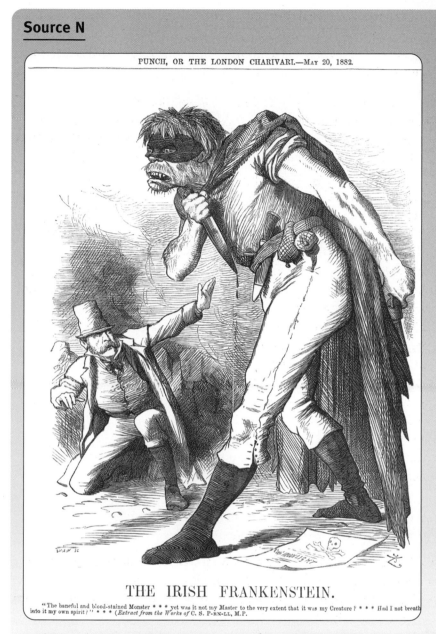

PUNCH, OR THE LONDON CHARIVARI.—May 20, 1882.

THE IRISH FRANKENSTEIN.

"The baneful and blood-stained Monster * * * yet was it not my Master to the very extent that it was my Creature? * * * Had I not breath into it my own spirit?" * * * (*Extract from the Works of C. S. P-RN-LL, M.P.*)

3.6 'The Irish Frankenstein' by John Tenniel published in *Punch*, 20 May 1882

The caption reads: 'The baneful and blood-stained Monster, *** yet was it not my Master to the very extent that it was my Creature? *** Had I not breathed into it my own spirit?' ***

SKILLS BUILDER

You should now be familiar with the drawings of John Tenniel. This cartoon is one of his most famous:

1 What are the messages of this cartoon?

2 How consistent is the depiction of the Irish in Source N with Tenniel's other cartoons (see pages 2, 44 and 46)?

Parnell's opportunity

The aftermath of the Phoenix Park Murders presented Parnell with a political opportunity that he was, as always, quick to seize. The temporary discrediting of the more violent strand of Irish nationalism allowed him to distance himself from the Fenians and Michael Davitt's radical proposals for land nationalisation. In October 1882, Parnell set up a new party, the Irish National League. The organisation's main aim was to work for Irish Home Rule. Parnell took the opportunity to impose greater discipline on the new party organisation. In 1884 the 'pledge' was introduced for all National League MPs. It committed them to vote with the party on all occasions if the majority of party members decided that they should do so. This gave Parnell considerable political power as party leader. Some more radical nationalists attacked Parnell's new organisation and leadership style.

Source O

[This was] the investing of the fortunes and guidance of the agitation, both for national self-government and land reform, in a leader's nominal dictatorship.

From Michael Davitt *The Fall of Feudalism in Ireland* published in 1904

Another view is as follows:

Source P

His creation of a disciplined, efficient and pledge-bound parliamentary party which by its performance at Westminster, offered a living proof that Ireland was ripe for self-government.

From F.S.L. Lyons *Ireland Since the Famine* pubilshed in 1971

SKILLS BUILDER

1 To what extent is Davitt's opinion in Source O a reliable assessment of the Irish National League? Use Source O and your own knowledge to explain your answer fully.

2 To what extent and why do Sources O and P differ in their conclusions.

Parnell's cause and that of his new party was greatly helped by reform of the franchise. Three pieces of legislation were make a significant difference:

- The Corrupt Practices Act 1883 set out the terms and conditions for party participation in elections.

- The Representation of the People Act 1884 extended the vote to the rural areas of Ireland by giving virtual manhood suffrage (the vote). The Irish electorate increased from 224,000 to 738,000.
- The Redistribution Act 1885 merged many borough seats into country seats.

The voters who were added to the register including many small tenant farmers and landless labourers who had previously been disenfranchised. These were the people who were to vote in huge numbers for the National League; their aspirations for a better life became bound up in a nationalist vision for the future of Ireland. Parnell continued to fuel their hopes for a better future, as in his speech in Cork on 21 January 1885, which was reported in *The Times* the following day. The speech is known as Parnell's '*ne plus ultra*' speech.

Definitions

'*Ne plus ultra*'
This means, in translation from Latin, 'no more beyond' (a certain point). In this context in means the ultimate goal of Irish nationalism.

Grattan's Parliament
is the name given to the Irish Parliament, which sat in the two decades up to the Act of Union of 1801.

Source Q

I do not know how this great question [of self-government] will be eventually settled. I do not know whether England will be wise in time and concede to constitutional arguments and methods the restitution of that which was stolen from us towards the close of the last century . . . and just as it is impossible for us to say in what way or by what means the National Question may be settled, in what ways full justice may be done in Ireland, so it cannot ask for anything less than **Grattan's Parliament**. No man has a right to say to his country 'Thus far shalt thou go and no further', and we have never attempted to fix the '*ne plus ultra*' to the progress of Ireland's nationhood, and we never shall.

From *The Times*, 22 January 1885

Parnell, ever the opportunist, courted the Catholic Church. Despite being a Protestant by birth and upbringing, he was prepared to woo the Catholic leadership by promising to support their demands to protect the Catholic education system. In 1884 Parnell condemned the Royal University set up by the 1879 Act and he vowed to protect the Catholic Church's control of education at all age levels. The following source is by the influential Archbishop of Dublin, William Walsh. He is speaking to an audience at a Catholic educational institution.

Source R

Politics now simply mean food and clothes and decent houses for Irishmen and women at home; they mean the protection of the weak against the strong, and the soil of Ireland for the Irish race rather than for a select gang of strangers and spoilers.

From Archbishop Walsh *United Ireland*, 21 November 1885

SKILLS BUILDER

1 What is implied in Parnell's comments in Source Q?

   When you are asked such a question, it is important that you do not simply write out what Parnell said. When you are asked what is implied, you are to try and get beneath the surface of the source and tease out what is inferred as well as what is stated.

2 What similarities are there between the message of Source Q and Source R?

The Gladstone government fell in June 1885 over a budget issue. As Ireland entered a period of relative peace, so Parnell courted and was courted by factions within the Liberal and Conservative parties keen to harness the Parliamentary power of the Irish Party:

- In 1884–85 Joseph Chamberlain of the Liberals tried to explore an agreement rooted in Irish support for the Liberals in return for reform of local government in Ireland. In the end the negotiating came to nothing.

- Despite significant hostility towards Home Rule, some Conservatives were prepared to at least talk to Parnell. On 1 August 1885, Parnell met with Tory peer Lord Carnarvon. Close agreement between the two parties was not likely, given the strength of Unionist sentiment on the Conservative back benches. However, Parnell was prepared to be wooed by the Conservatives and he encouraged Irish voters on mainland Britain to vote for Conservative Party candidates in the November–December 1885 General Election. The importance for Parnell of the Conservative Party was that they held sway in the House of Lords and would, therefore, be the only party who could realistically deliver the constitutional reform hoped for by Parnell.

In the election, Parnell's Home Rulers won eighty-six seats and they held the balance of power; the Liberals holding an eighty-five seat majority over the Conservatives. Parnell was at the peak of his influence.

SKILLS BUILDER

What does Source S suggest are the concerns in Ulster regarding Home Rule?

Definition

Protective Tariffs

These are taxes imposed on imports. Such taxes would benefit Irish agriculture but not industry.

Case study: the Unionist response to Parnell

For much of the last unit and this, we have focused on those in Ireland who wanted to weaken the union between Britain and Ireland. However, it is important to keep an eye on those who wanted to retain the Union. Events surrounding by-elections in Monaghan and Fermanagh in the north in 1883 showed the strength of feeling against Parnell in some sections of Irish society. Even though Parnell's party managed to win the Monaghan by-election and some seats in Ulster in the 1885 General Election, there were many in that province and other parts of Ireland who had become threatened by the emergence of Parnell and the calls for Home Rule. Here is an historian's view of the tension in Ulster in the early 1880s.

Source S

Ulster's forms of sectarian and Unionist politics, already in existence, were set hard by the dynamic political events of the 1880s. Despite a tradition of Tenant Right agitation, and an early commitment to the Land League programme in several Ulster countries, the Land League was rapidly perceived as a nationalist front and the Orange Order took a strong anti-league line. The notion of Parnellism 'invading' Ulster was particularly potent and it resulted in violent incidents in Monaghan and Fermanagh during 1883.

Adapted from R.F. Foster *Modern Ireland 1600–1972* published in 1988

Below are two contemporary sources, one from 1883, the other from 1884. The drawing is from the weekly magazine *Moonshine*, which was published between 1879 and 1900. The picture in question was drawn by famous cartoonist John Proctor.

Source T

If the government fail to prevent Mr Parnell and Co. from making inroads into Ulster if they do not prevent those hordes of ruffians from invading us, we will take the law into our own hands.

Unionist landlord and MP for Liverpool Lord Claud Hamilton, 1883

Source U

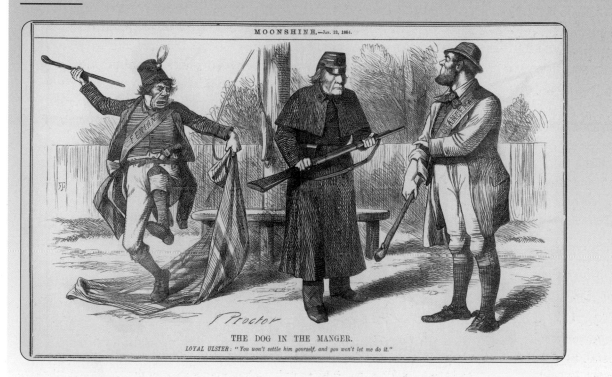

3.7 'Orange and Fenian' drawn by John Proctor, published in *Moonshine* on 12 January 1884. The caption reads 'Loyal Ulster: "You won't settle him yourself, and you won't let me do it".'

Unit summary

What have you learned in this unit?

Irish politics had changed considerably from the mid-1860s to 1885. The threat of Fenianism was secondary in significance to the emergence of a more coherent form of Irish nationalism based on the demand for Home Rule. The impact of the challenge posed by both strands of nationalism was to change the British political landscape. It was also to provoke the emergence of a more strident unionism based in the north of Ireland.

What skills have you used in this unit?

You will have used a range of evidence to explore the issues relating to Home Rule, Fenianism and unionism up to 1885. You will have used cartoons as part of your enquiry primarily to inform about prevalent popular attitudes towards the Irish. You have tested a number of sources through evaluating their reliability and you will have cross-referenced sources for information.

SKILLS BUILDER

1 You have used a number of pieces of pictorial evidence in this unit. Working in pairs, consider the benefits to the historian of being able to use such information.

2 Select any five sources from the unit. How far does the evidence suggest that the cause of Home Rule was, by 1885, an impossible one?

3 Put all the political figures mentioned in this unit in an imaginary balloon. Organise a balloon debate, matching a student with each political figure, and with the student speaking out in defence of his/her chosen political figure. Who is left in the balloon? Why?

Exam tips

- Get underneath the sources and make **inferences** from them.
- **Compare** the sources by analysing their similarities and differences.
- **Contextualise** the sources, giving weight to the significance of their origin, nature and purpose.
- Reach a **judgement** on 'How far' by using the sources as a set.

Remember, there is the Exam zone section at the end of the book to help you further.

Exam style questions

This is the sort of question you will find appearing on the examination paper as an (a) question.

Study Sources C, D and E.

How far do Sources C and E support the view of the Fenians as expressed in Source D?

You tackled an (a) type question at the end of Unit 1. Look back at the exam tips you were given there on page 16. Now is the time to consolidate those tips. What do you have to do to write a successful answer to an (a) type question?

Now plan an answer to this question and write a response.

RESEARCH TOPIC

Belfast

The economy of most of Ireland at this time was agricultural. However, Belfast and other towns in Ulster were transformed by industrial development. Your task is to use all the different resources that you can to find out about the growth in industry that took place in Belfast. You are to focus on the following features:

- shipbuilding;

- the linen industry;

- how industrialisation had an impact on local politics.

Home Rule and opposition, 1886–1905

What is this unit about?

This unit focuses on the arguments for and against Home Rule for Ireland. It also looks at alternative strategies adopted by the British government for solving the Irish Question. The unit covers the career of Charles Stewart Parnell and, after the defeat of Home Rule attempts at 'killing Home Rule with kindness', you will:

- find out how Home Rule was proposed and denied;
- work with source material to evaluate the nature of the campaign for Home Rule and the reasons why it was opposed and failed.

Key questions

- Why were two Home Rule Bills introduced, one in 1886, the other in 1893?
- What was the impact on Irish affairs of certain individuals including William Gladstone, Charles Stewart Parnell, Joseph Chamberlain, Arthur Balfour and Charles Wyndham?

Timeline

1885

January	Parnell's 'ne plus ultra' speech
June	Redistribution of Seats Act changes constituency divisions
August	Ashbourne Act: land purchase extended
December	Hawarden Kite: Gladstone's conversion to Home Rule

1886

April	First Home Rule Bill introduced
June	Home Rule Bill defeated
October	Launch of the 'Plan of Campaign'

1887

March	Arthur Balfour appointed Chief Secretary of Ireland
September	Mitchelstown Massacre

1889   Pigott exposed as forger, O'Shea divorce petition

1890   Parnell ousted as leader of the Irish Party

1891

February	'The Split' of the Irish Party
August	Land Purchase Act
October	Death of Parnell

1893

February	Second Home Bill introduced
September	Second Home Bill rejected by the House of Lords

1896	Balfour's Land Act
1900	
January	Reunification of Irish Party
November	George Wyndham appointed Chief Secretary of Ireland
1902	Land Conference
1903	Wyndham's Land Act
1905	
March	Ulster Unionist Council set up
March	George Wyndham resigns

The *Whitehall Review* was a popular weekly newspaper published in Victorian London. It covered political affairs as well as financial and society news. The artist commissioned to make this drawing has a clear point to make about Home Rule.

SKILLS BUILDER

What is the point the artist is trying to make?

How accurate a summary is this of the state of Home Rule in mid-1885?

Source A

"St. Stephen's Review" Presentation Cartoon, May 23rd, 1885.

FORGOTTEN.

(WITH APOLOGIES TO J. S. NOBLE)

4.1 'Forgotten' published in the *Whitehall Review* in May 1885. The horse has 'Home Trade' written on its side.

What exactly was Home Rule?

From 1880, Charles Parnell was leader of the Irish Party that campaigned for Home Rule for Ireland. However, one of the ambiguities of Home Rule and Charles Parnell's position in 1885 was that Home Rule could be interpreted in a number of ways:

- Gladstone did not like the term 'Home Rule' instead using 'local autonomy', which meant that Ireland would have a fair degree of self-government. Both he and the majority of his party saw 'Home Rule' as placing Ireland in the same relationship as Canada.

- Gladstone also drew parallels between the position of Norway in relation to Sweden, the former recognising the Swedish Crown in return for a significant degree of autonomy.

- To others within the Liberal Party, however, 'Home Rule' should and could be no more than greater administrative devolution; that is, that Ireland would not have its own government but more administration of Irish affairs, for example, tax offices would be based in Ireland rather than in England.

Parnell's 'ne plus ultra' speech of 21 January 1885 (see page 55) is a good example of the ambiguity of Home Rule. The fact that questions exist explains the emotion and tension that the issue raised. Although much debated, the following questions were not answered with enough clarity and confidence to allay fears of Unionists:

- Did Home Rule mean Ireland would ultimately stay within the Empire, or was it the first step on the road to separatism?

- Would Home Rule be enough to deal with the Irish Question or was it a means to an end?

- What would become of Ulster?

Why did Gladstone introduce the First Home Rule Bill?

On 17 December 1885, just as the General Election results were still trickling in, the press dropped a political bombshell, the so-called **Hawarden Kite**. For over a year, Parnell had dallied with both Conservative and Liberal parties. As the election results were declared in December 1885, it became clear that Parnell's followers were to hold the balance of power in the House of Commons. It was also becoming clear that, despite the discussions between Parnell and the Conservative Lord Lieutenant of Ireland Lord Carnarvon in the summer of 1885, the Conservative Party was not prepared to entertain Home Rule. One hope for Gladstone may well have been a bi-partisan approach, with both major parties backing some form of Home Rule. Gladstone's hand was forced however, by the actions of his son and Private Secretary, Herbert, who leaked the following information in Source B to the press.

Definition

Hawarden Kite

The term to 'fly a kite' is used in politics when a politician raises an idea via the media with the intention of gauging reaction to that idea. Hawarden was the name of Gladstone's home.

Questions

1 Why, does the newspaper suggest, is Mr Gladstone in favour of Home Rule?

2 To what extent does the Hawarden Kite represent a political triumph for Parnell?

Source B

Mr Gladstone has definitely adopted the policy of Home Rule for Ireland and there are well-founded hopes that he will win over the chief representatives of the moderate section of his party to his views.

Mr Gladstone is sanguine that the policy of settling the Irish question once and for all will commend itself to the majority of his party and to the English people, when it is clearly understood that no other course can bring real peace. If he is enabled to eject the government on this issue, he will have a large majority in the House of Commons for his Irish bill and he believes that the House of Lords, weighing the gravity of the situation, will not reject it.

There is reasonable expectation that both Lord Hartington and Mr Goschen will come round to Mr Gladstone's view, and Mr Chamberlain and Sir Charles Dilke, In spite of their recent attitude, could not consistently oppose it.

Pall Mall Gazette, 'Hawarden Kite' published on 17 December 1885

So what had brought Gladstone to Home Rule?

The results of the 1885 election gave out a very clear message. In 1880 the Liberals had won 13 seats in Ireland, in 1885 they won none (the Conservatives holding on to 19 out of 26 seats). What became clear from the election results of 1885 was the strength of support for Parnell's party. Not only did the Irish Party win 85 out of the 103 seats in Ireland (plus one in Liverpool), they also won many of the seats with huge majorities. The examples of the landslide for the Irish Party were many; in wealthy County Kilkenny (which returned two MPs), both nationalist candidates scored over 4,000 votes with the two Conservative candidates scoring 220 and 170 votes, respectively. Above all else, Gladstone feared that the strength of the nationalist vote might lead the nationalists to decide to set up their own Parliament in Dublin.

What was the impact on the Liberal Party?

The fallout from the first Home Rule Bill was to shape British politics for the next two decades. Just as Gladstone's idol, Sir Robert Peel, had split his party over the introduction of the Corn Laws in 1846, so Gladstone's decision had torn apart the Liberal Party. In some senses, this split had been long coming. This is the view of one of Gladstone's more recent biographers:

Source C

Gladstone's fundamental weakness was that he was trying to hold together too wide a coalition. His social conservatism had come in uncomfortable conflict with his political radicalism. He was willing to make a great effort to keep the traditional Whig families within the Liberal tabernacle. The problem was that, as the issues of the 1880s evolved, even before Home Rule appeared like a dividing spear, there had ceased to be any significant disputes on which men like Hartington and Argyll were instinctively on the progressive side of the watershed.

From Roy Jenkins *Gladstone: A Biography* published in 1997

The wing of the Liberal Party led by Lord Hartington stood resolutely against Home Rule because they believed that it undermined the concept of Empire. As Roy Jenkins suggested in Source C, the Whigs had become increasingly concerned about the radicalism of Gladstonian liberalism. They had disliked the implications of successive Irish Land Acts that had challenged property rights and they feared that Home Rule would do the same. Indeed, their suspicions were seemingly confirmed when Gladstone proposed to link Home Rule to a land purchase measure.

Biography

Joseph Chamberlain (1836–1914)

Joseph Chamberlain was born in London in 1836 and became one of the most prominent politicians of his generation as a Liberal and then Conservative MP and minister. Chamberlain first entered into politics as a Liberal, served as a reforming mayor of Birmingham before being elected as one of the city's MPs in 1876. He soon was promoted, becoming President of the Board of Trade in the government of William Ewart Gladstone in 1880. Chamberlain was a strong supporter of Land Reform in Ireland, believing that reform was the best way to deflect the demands for Home Rule. Chamberlain's opposition to Home Rule came from a deep seated belief that Home Rule for Ireland would lead to the disintegration of the United Kingdom and, eventually, the Empire. However, he was in favour of discussion and debate with Irish nationalists and, to that end, he brokered the 'Kilmainham Treaty' in 1882. Chamberlain's interest in Irish politics remained, despite being overlooked by Gladstone for the post of Chief Secretary in Ireland (the position was offered to Sir George Trevelyan instead). In 1885 he put forward the idea of limited devolution of powers through the creation of the Irish Central Board to deal with issues such as education and land. The idea was rejected by Cabinet and dismissed by Parnell.

In the run-up to the 1885 General Election, Chamberlain devised the *Radical Programme* that called for, amongst other things, more direct taxation, land and education reform, the disestablishment of the Church and universal male suffrage.

Despite Liberal victory in the 1885 election, Chamberlain resigned from the party in March 1886 once Gladstone made clear his plans for Home Rule. Throughout the election campaign, Chamberlain had argued that Ireland had as much right to autonomy and self-government as London. Chamberlain moved, with his Whig allies led by Lord Hartington to set up the Liberal Unionist Association that set up electoral links with the Conservative Party. For a number of years, Chamberlain remained in political isolation despite strong links with the more radical conservatives such as Lord Randolph Churchill. However, he joined the Conservative government in 1895 as Colonial Secretary. For the next few years he was a ferocious supporter of Empire and managed to split the Conservative Party over the issue of free trade (Chamberlain supporting the idea of protectionism within the Empire). Chamberlain suffered a stroke in 1906, retired from politics and died in 1914.

Perhaps the most telling opposition from within the Liberal Party came from Joseph Chamberlain. His opposition to Home Rule was not rooted in a belief that there should be no reform in Ireland. Chamberlain had himself suggested administrative reform as a means of dealing with the Irish Question. In 1885 numerous statements made by Chamberlain had given an ambiguous message.

Source D

[We should meet] in the fullest possible way the legitimate aspirations of the Irish people towards entire independence in the management of their local affairs.

The Central Board [for Ireland] will only be the Metropolitan Board of Works on a larger and more important scale.

From Joseph Chamberlain *The Irish Question* published in 1885

Question

How far do these statements agree and what is are the limitations of Chamberlain's proposals?

In the end Chamberlain opposed Home Rule on the grounds that it went further than the administrative solution he had proposed in 1885. He also believed that to propose a Home Rule settlement independent of a review of the United Kingdom as a whole was unwise and would, in time, lead to the unravelling of the Union. Chamberlain resigned from the Cabinet on 13 March. Other radical members of the party, such as John Bright, who had been sympathetic to the Irish cause, baulked at Home Rule as suggested by Gladstone.

Conservative opposition

The impact of the Hawarden Kite was to reinforce the Conservative position against Home Rule. Conservative opposition to Home Rule was based on a number of points. The Conservative leader, Lord Salisbury, saw political opportunity. Conservative divisions in 1832 and 1867 over reform of the franchise and in 1846 over Repeal of the Corn Laws subsequently led to long periods of Whig or Liberal rule. Above all else, Conservative opposition was based on a belief that Home Rule would lead to the break up of the union and an undermining of Empire.

What were the Home Rule proposals?

Gladstone presented the Home Rule Bill into the House of Commons on 8 April 1886 and the Land Purchase Bill on 16 April 1886. He spoke at length, detailing his proposals. Below are adapted extracts from Gladstone's speech.

Questions

1 What are the main arguments of Gladstone's speech?
2 What is the significance of his reference to 'reconstruction of administrative government?'

Source E

While I think it is right to modify the Union in some particulars, we are not about to prepare its repeal. A supreme statutory authority of the Imperial Parliament over Great Britain, Scotland and Ireland, as one United Kingdom, was established by the Act of Union. That supreme authority is not intended in the slightest degree to impair.

[There are] gentlemen of very high authority, who are strongly opposed to giving Ireland a domestic legislature, have said nevertheless that they think that there might be a general reconstruction of the administrative government in Ireland. The fault of the administrative system of Ireland is that its spring . . . its motor muscle . . . is English and not Irish. The settlement of this issue is the establishment by authority of Parliament, of a legislative body sitting in Dublin for the conduct of both legislation and administration under the conditions which may be prescribed by the Act defining Irish, as distinct from Imperial affairs.

I cannot conceal the conviction that the voice of Ireland, as a whole, is at the moment clearly and constitutionally spoken. I cannot say it is otherwise when five-sixths of its lawfully chosen representatives are of one mind in this matter. There is a counter voice [but] I cannot allow it to be said that a Protestant minority in Ulster or elsewhere is to rule the question at large in Ireland. But I do think that the Protestant minority should have its wishes considered to the utmost practicable extent in any form which they may assume.

Irish nationality vents itself in the demand for local autonomy or separate and complete self-government in Irish affairs. The Irishman is profoundly Irish, but it does not follow that because his local patriotism is keen he is incapable of Imperial patriotism.

William Gladstone speaking in the House of Commons, 8 April 1886

What did the Home Rule Bill propose?

The main features of Gladstone's Home Rule Bill were:

- Ireland was to be granted an Assembly but with two Orders of representatives: one Order with 28 peers and 75 members elected by the propertied classes, the other with 204 elected members. The Orders could meet together or apart.
- The Imperial Parliament at Westminster was to retain control over issues relating to defence, Empire and the Crown.
- Executive power was to be exercised by the Lord Lieutenant who was not answerable to either Order.
- The Irish Parliament would levy its own direct taxes to fund Home Rule. Income from Irish Customs and Excise would go to the London Treasury to pay for Ireland's contribution to Empire and the National Debt. Ireland's contribution was to be £3,242,000.
- There would be no Irish MPs at Westminster despite the fact that Westminster still retained control over various aspects of Irish taxation.

Case study: What were the reactions to Gladstone's proposals?

It would be best to let those for and against Home Rule speak for themselves. As you read through these next sources, think not only about the reasons they are giving, but also about the time they were writing or drawing.

Source F

AN "EXIT" SPEECH.

"THE REST, THAT LOVE ME, RISE AND FOLLOW *ME*."—*Richard the Third*, Act III., Sc. iv.

4.2 Cartoon by John Tenniel called *An 'Exit' Speech* published in *Punch*, 22 May 1886.

Gladstone is shown as being isolated and unpopular in his arguments over the Irish Question.

Source G

Home Rule will send a quickening stir of grateful life through a discontented land, which has long been rent with civil feuds. It will dress the labourer's face with smiles, lift him in the scale of civilisation, imbue him with the true spirit of human toil. It will educate and enrich him.

Joseph Cowan MP speaking in the House of Commons, *Hansard*, May 1886

Source H

4.3 The front page of the *Illustrated London News* from 1881. It shows Home Rulers in the House of Commons supporting Gladstone and calling for the release of Michael Davitt. The caption reads 'The Home Rulers stood up and for some time with raised hands shouted "privilege"'.

Source I

Downing Street. Long interview for 2 hours with Mr Gladstone at his request . . . He explained much of his policy as to a Dublin Parliament. At to Land Purchase, I objected to the land policy as unnecessary . . . As to a Dublin Parliament, I argued that he was making a surrender all along the line. A Dublin Parliament would work with constant friction, and would press against any barrier he might keep to keep up the unity of the 3 kingdoms.

What of a volunteer force and what of import duties and protection against us as British officers? He would not object, but any armed force must be under officers appointed by the Crown.

I told him to get rid of the Irishmen from Westminster, such as we have known them for 5 or 6 years past, would do something to make his propositions less offensive and distasteful in Great Britain tho' it tends to separation.

I thought he placed far too much confidence in the leaders of the Rebel Party. I could place none in them and the general feeling was and is that any terms with them would not be kept.

From John Bright *Extracts From My Diary* written on 20 March 1886

Source J

Our capital under a Home Rule government would be induced to flow, for we should have industry and trade. We would bring all the resources of the country into play, as to Irish fisheries, piers, harbours, canals, navigation, roads – in fact with regard to almost everything concerning the internal traffic and life of the country . . . it will not be a Parliament of politicians, but one of earnest, energetic, practical men, anxious to restore the prosperity of their country.

From a speech by Justin MacCarthy MP of the Irish Party to the House of Commons, May 1886. Reported by *Hansard*.

Source K

All Mr Gladstone's policy . . . since 1880 has been a policy of concession to the party of Mr Parnell, to weaken the power of the Loyalists and strengthen that of the disloyal party . . . If political parties and political leaders . . . should be so utterly lost to every feeling and dictate of honour and courage as to hand over coldly, and for the sake of purchasing a short an illusory Parliamentary tranquillity, the lives and liberties of the Loyalists of Ireland to their hereditary and bitter foes, make no doubt on this point – Ulster will not be a consenting party; Ulster at the proper moment will resort to . . . force: Ulster will fight, Ulster will be right . . .

From a speech to Unionists by Lord Randolph Churchill, Ulster Hall, Belfast, 22 February 1886

Source L

In America or Switzerland federalism has developed because existing states wished to be combined into some kind of national unity . . . The vast majority of the United Kingdom, including a million or more of the inhabitants of Ireland, have expressed their will to maintain the Union. Popular government means government in accordance with the will of the people . . . Their wish is decisive, and ought to terminate the whole agitation in favour of Home Rule.

From A.V. Dicey *England's Case Against Home Rule* published in 1886

SKILLS BUILDER

After studying Sources F to L, answer the following questions:

1 What are the arguments expressed for and against Home Rule?

2 Source I is a significant source:

 Why are John Bright's words so important?

3 Source H has an incomplete attribution in that we do not know who drew the source and we do not know the exact date when it was drawn. Does this matter?

Defeat of the Bill

Given the weight of opposition on the Liberal benches to the Home Rule Bill, it was little surprise that at the end of May, Joseph Chamberlain and around fifty Liberal MPs agreed to vote against the Bill at its **Second Reading**.

- The Bill was defeated by thirty votes, Gladstone resigned as Prime Minister.
- A General Election was called; Chamberlain and his fellow Liberal Unionists did well, gaining 77 seats, the Conservatives also performing well with 316 seats.
- The Gladstone Liberals were reduced to a rump of 192 seats.
- The vote and number of seats for the Irish Party remained similar to the 1885 election.

The picture below was published in the *St Stephen's Review of Facts and Fancies, Thoughts, Realities and Shams*. The magazine was published under this name from 1883 to 1892. Tom Merry was a very well known political cartoonist and satirist.

Source M

THE HOME RULE LEAP

4.4 *The Home Rule Leap* by Tom Merry published in *St Stephen's Review,* 4 September 1886.

What was the Unionist reaction?

Many within the Protestant minority in Ireland did not want to participate in an Assembly dominated by the Catholic majority. The Home Rule debate in London was accompanied by ferocious sectarian rioting in Belfast, which left 32 dead and 371 wounded. At this point, most northern unionists considered themselves as 'loyal' to the Crown but Irish. The General Election of 1886 was to provide telling evidence that the strength of Irish unionism lay in the north. In Ulster, sixteen seats were won by the nationalists and fifteen seats were won by the Unionists. In the rest of the country, the Unionists won two seats and the nationalists won sixty-eight seats. The dividing lines between unionist Ulster and the rest of Ireland were becoming clearer.

Discussion point

In pairs or in groups, study Merry's picture in Source M and answer the following questions:

- What are the conclusions to draw from the picture?
- How appropriate and accurate is Merry's drawing?

Source N

You must give up the idea of protecting the Protestants either as a body or as a majority by the establishment of a separate legislature either in Ulster or in any portion of Ulster. No, sir, we can not give up a single Irishman. We want the energy, the patriotism, the talents, and the work of every Irishman to insure that this great experiment shall be a successful one. We want, sir, all creeds and all classes in Ireland. We can not consent to look upon a single Irishman as not belonging to us.

We do not blame the small proportion of the Protestants of Ireland who feel any real fear. I admit, sir, that there is a small proportion of them who do feel this fear. We do not blame them; we have been doing our best to allay that fear, and we shall continue to do so. Theirs is not the shame and disgrace of this fear. That shame and disgrace belong to right honourable gentlemen and noble lords of English political parties who, for selfish interests, have sought to rekindle the embers – the almost expiring embers – of religious bigotry.

Parnell's speech to the House of Commons, Second Reading of the Irish Home Rule Bill reported in *The Times*, 8 June 1886

Coercion

In a speech to the House of Lords in June 1886 the leader of the Conservative Party, Lord Salisbury, outlined the position of his party with regards to Ireland.

Source O

The object of my observations was to show that the application of the word 'coercion' to the measures recommended by us was wholly unsuitable and improper; and coercion, according to the ordinary use of the term, means legislation in restraint of liberty and directed against political disaffection . . . What we have desired to recommend is legislation in protection of liberty – legislation to defend the innocent population against the unlawful acts of criminal men and criminal associations. This has never been called coercion . . . it ought to be recommended, not only for twenty years, but for ever, and not only in Ireland but in every civilised country.

Lord Salisbury speaking in the House of Lords, 4 June 1886, reported by *Hansard*

The 'Plan of Campaign' launched in 1886 threatened to lead to another Land War. The response of Lord Salisbury's government was a policy of coercion and reform; the aim of the latter to 'kill Home Rule with kindness'. The architect to this new policy in Ireland was the Chief Secretary Arthur James Balfour. From taking office in March 1887 to his departure from Ireland in 1892, Balfour acted with ruthlessness and efficiency. His work was made easier by the passing of the Perpetual Crimes Act (1887) (Coercion Act) which, and this was new, was a permanent piece of legislation that did not have to be renewed annually. It allowed for imprisonment of those agitating for land reform by using boycotts, rent strikes and so forth. The police were given greater powers as was witnessed at the Mitchelstown Massacre in September 1887 when three protestors were shot dead by the Royal Irish Constabulary. The view expressed in the nationalist *The Weekly Freeman* stands as evidence to the impact of the government's tactics. The British government succeeded in persuading Pope Leo XIII to condemn the tactics of the Plan of Campaign in May 1886.

Source P

SUPPLEMENT GIVEN AWAY WITH THE **WEEKLY FREEMAN** 23RD JULY, 1887.   PRICE THREE HALF-PENCE

THE LION 'TORY.' DANGEROUS

IN THE LION'S DEN.
(After the celebrated picture by GABRIEL MAX.)
Erin has been dragged into the Tory Den, but happily there is an ardent admirer not far off.

4.5 'In the Lion's Den', *The Weekly Freeman*, 23 July 1887.

A somewhat different line was taken by Tom Merry. In Source Q opposite, Balfour is shown as a modern day Perseus rescuing Andromeda (Perseus was a hero of Greek legend. One of his great deeds was to rescue princess and future wife Andromeda from a sea monster).

Source Q

4.6 *Balfour Rescues Erin [Ireland]* by Tom Merry in the *St Stephens Review*, 16 March 1889.

The end of Parnell

From 1886 Parnell and his party were tied to the Liberals. Instead of having the flexibility of being able to play off the two leading parties against each other, Parnell's opportunities for political manoeuvring were now far more limited. Parnell also faced the challenge of the more radical element of Irish nationalism. The emergence of the 'Plan of Campaign' in October 1886 (see page 34) threatened to undermine Parnell's position as a central, and increasingly respectable figure, at the heart of the parliamentary political system. His reputation was to be enhanced and then destroyed by a quite extraordinary series of events. As part of a campaign to 'smear' Parnell's political reputation by making him seem sympathetic to violent nationalism, *The Times* newspaper printed a series of letters in 1887 and 1888, supposedly written by Parnell.

SKILLS BUILDER

Why and how do Sources P and Q give different impressions about Britain's policy towards Ireland in the years between 1886 and 1890?

Discussion point

Think of other attempts that you have seen so far in this book, to discredit Parnell by linking him to violence. Why do you think that there were such attempts to damage the reputation of Parnell?

Source R

In concluding our series of articles on 'Parnellism and Crime' we intimated that unpublished evidence existed which would bind still closer the links between the 'constitutional chiefs and the contrivers of murder and outrage' . . . We do not think it right to withhold any longer from public knowledge the fact that we possess and have had in our custody for some time documentary evidence which has a most serious bearing on the Parnellite conspiracy, and which, after a most careful and minute scrutiny is, we are satisfied, quite authentic.

From *The Times* newspaper, 1887

In February 1889, the letters were proved, by a Special Commission, to be the work of a forger, Richard Piggot. Parnell rode high on a wave of Liberal sympathy. He met with Gladstone and even courted the Conservatives over land reform. Parnell's downfall came not because of the actions of his political enemies but because of his private life. In November 1890, Captain O'Shea petitioned for divorce from his wife naming Parnell in his divorce petition. Victorian society was offended, the non-conformist base of the Liberal party, Home Rulers such as Hugh Price Hughes, condemned Parnell as an adulterer as did the Catholic Church. Below are two sources of evidence summarising the reaction to the court case:

Source S

Mr Dear Morley,

Having arrived at a certain conclusion with regard to the continuance of Mr Parnell's leadership of the Irish Party . . . I thought it necessary to acquaint Mr McCarthy [Irish Party MP Justin McCarthy] with the conclusion at which I had arrived. It was not withstanding the splendid service rendered by Mr Parnell to his country, his continuance at the present moment in the leadership would be productive of consequences disastrous in the highest degree to the cause of Ireland.

A letter from Gladstone to his close political confidant John Morley, 24 November 1890

Source T

SKILLS BUILDER

1 What do Sources S and T show about the relationship between Parnell and the Liberal Party in 1890?

2 How far do these sources agree?

3 Which of these two sources is the more reliable in its account of relations between Parnell and Gladstone in late 1890?

"SEPARATISTS."

Douglas . . . . Mr. Gl-dst-ne.   Marmion . . . . Mr. P-rn-ll.

Douglas. "THE HAND OF DOUGLAS IS HIS OWN;
AND NEVER SHALL IN FRIENDLY GRASP
THE HAND OF SUCH AS MARMION CLASP!"—*Marmion, Canto VI.*

4.7 Engraving by John Swain in *Punch* magazine, December 1890 with the title *Gladstone and Parnell.*

Biography

John Redmond

John Redmond was born in a Catholic gentry family in Wexford in September 1856. After university he worked as a clerk in the House of Commons before being elected an MP in 1881. He took part in the Land War (1879–82) and Plan of Campaign (1886–91) but was deeply opposed to the use of physical force. Indeed Redmond was committed to political change by constitutional means. He sought Home Rule but did not want to see Ireland leave the Empire. Redmond took the leadership of the minority pre-Parnell group in Parliament after Parnell was forced from the leadership of the Irish Party in 1890. In 1900 he became leader of the reunified movement despite opposition from William O'Brien and Tim Healy. The elections of 1910 provided Redmond with the opportunity to persuade Herbert Asquith to introduce a Bill to introduce the third Home Rule Bill in April 1912. Redmond's actions are covered in some detail in Unit 5.

When war broke out in 1914, Redmond encouraged Irish support for Britain. He also tried to persuade the government that Ireland should be guarded by the Volunteers, north and south, so that British troops could be redeployed to the continent. Redmond refused a place in the War Cabinet in 1915 and was devastated by the Easter Rising of 1916. In 1917 he persuaded the Prime Minister of the time, David Lloyd George, to call a Convention to discuss the constitutional future of Ireland. He did not live to see the outcome of the Convention, dying on 6 March 1918.

What was 'the Split'?

A meeting of seventy-three MPs of the Irish Party in December 1890 ended in schism; Parnellites against anti-Parnellites. Parnell was bitterly attacked by many MPs, most notably Tim Healy. At the end of the meeting, Justin McCarthy and forty-four other MPs seceded from the party. Parnell was supported by the Fenians and urban based MPs. Parnell threw himself into three by-election campaigns in 1891; his platform being noticeably more radical and Fenian in its content and tone. In reality he was a broken man politically and emotionally and he died in Brighton in 1891. It was not just Parnell the man who was broken by 'the Split'; the Parnellite coalition, which he so successfully managed and held together, broke apart in acrimony and bitterness. Until 1900 the Irish Party fragmented into two main camps:

- Irish National League led by John Redmond.

- Irish National Federation eventually led by John Dillon but containing a number of prominent politicians including William O'Brien and Tim Healy.

Discussion points

Charles Stewart Parnell
In the Skills Builder section at the end of this unit, there is a debate set up for you to argue whether Parnell was a failure or not. At this point, it would be useful for you to reflect on Parnell's political career.

In your groups, come up with a list of questions about Parnell to discuss: here are two examples:

- How far should Parnell be judged a political opportunist?

- How far was Parnell, at heart, a Fenian?

Once you have come up with a list of questions, you and your group should pick the ones you think are most interesting and should discuss them.

Gladstone's progress

The most popular book in Britain in the nineteenth century, bar the Bible, was the *Pilgrim's Progress* written by John Bunyan. One of the places that Christian, the pilgrim, passes through is the Valley of the Shadow of Death. In the book, the Valley is described as very dangerous with a quicksand bog on one side of the road and a deep ditch on the other side. Although it is not very likely that many people would recognise that the cartoon below is based on the story of *Pilgrim's Progress*, the vast majority of people in the nineteenth century would have recognised it straight away.

Source U

A PILGRIM'S PROGRESS.

4.8 From *Punch Almanac*, April 1893, 'Home Rule: Ulster Last Ditch'.

What did the Second Home Rule Bill (1893) propose?

Despite the fall of Parnell, Gladstone and the Liberal Party were still wedded to the idea of Home Rule. During the General Election campaign of 1892, Gladstone campaigned on the issue of Irish Home Rule and, including the votes of Irish Home Rulers, the Liberals had a majority of forty votes. A new Home Rule Bill was introduced into the House of Commons in the summer of 1893. It inspired the usual passionate debate;

indeed emotions ran so high that at the end of the debate on the Second Reading there was a mass punch-up on the floor of the House of Commons involving forty or so MPs! The Bill was passed by a majority of thirty-four votes on the Third Reading:

- The Bill proposed an Irish Assembly consisting of an upper house (48 members) and a lower house (103 members), both of which were to be elected.
- Executive power would reside with the Lord Lieutenant who would form a Privy Council.
- The Second Home Rule Bill differed from the First Home Rule Bill in that eighty Irish MPs would remain at Westminster and would be able to vote on Bills relating to Ireland.
- Ireland was to contribute one-third of her revenue to the Imperial Exchequer.
- Judges were to be appointed by the Irish government.

The House of Lords were not of the same opinion and the Bill was voted down by 419 votes to 41.

What was Constructive Unionism?

Arthur Balfour's term of office in Ireland as Chief Secretary and that of his brother Gerald (Chief Secretary from 1895 to 1900) was not one of coercion alone. Indeed, another consequence of the debate over Home Rule was a change in policy and tactics of Conservative governments onwards. This was driven in part by an understanding that reform, rather than coercion, would in the long run strengthen the Union. A number of politicians are linked with this philosophy, notably the Liberal Unionist MP, Horace Plunkett. The term used by many historians to describe Conservative tactics is 'Constructive Unionism'. This is accurate to the extent that the policies were constructive. The main motivation behind the policies was to strengthen the union by attempting to make economic conditions in Ireland similar to the rest of the United Kingdom. Whether this was the best policy was yet to be seen. There are some of the reforms introduced:

Land reforms

Without doubt the most significant aspect of 'Constructive Unionism' was land reform. This has been explained in some detail in Unit 2 (see pages 18 36). Land purchase Acts in 1887, 1891 and 1896 built on the legislation of 1885 in providing loans for tenants to buy land. The 1891 Act made £33 million available, and some 55,000 tenants took advantage of the proposals.

Congested District Boards 1891

The Boards were set up as part of the 1891 Land Act. They constituted an imaginative approach to the economic problems that were specific in the west of Ireland. The Boards helped resettle people from over- to under-populated regions. It also built new houses where necessary, up to 3,000 in total. It also promoted rural industry such as fishing or the production of Donegal tweed. By 1923 the Congested District Boards had bought and had handed out over 2 million acres.

Recess Committee 1895–96

The cross party committee was set up under the direction of Horace Plunkett. Its brief was to look at ways of improving Irish agriculture. In 1899 an Irish Department of Agriculture and Technical Instruction was established. An aim of the Department was to promote new methods of farming. Plunkett won some admirers for his work although he found it difficult to persuade farmers to change their ways.

All-Ireland Committee 1897

This committee was set up as a cross party committee and individuals on the committee represented a range of opinion from the nationalist John Redmond to staunch unionists such as Colonel Edward Saunderson.

Source V

Sir Horace Plunkett's policy and that of the wise and able men who have worked and are working with him, may briefly be described as the strengthening and development of the Irish character by the promotion of self-help primarily through association, and then through Government aid and guidance, strictly seeking the promotion and avoiding the impairment of self help. In this direction very much has been done and Sir Horace regards the future, though complex and difficult, as extremely hopeful.

By Edward Cary reviewing Sir Horace Plunkett's book '*Ireland in the New Century*', published in the *New York Times*, 2 April 1904

Local Government (Ireland) Act, 1898

Instead of local government being controlled by Protestant landowners through grand juries, the Act fully reformed Irish local government. The importance of this reform is well summarised in the following source.

Source W

The new local-government system had both a financial and a political importance. Under the terms of the new act, local government was now to be made up of county councils, urban and rural district councils and boards of guardians. As a result of the Act, male householders and those occupying part of a house now had the vote. From the first elections held in April 1899 onwards there was a greater opportunity for nationalist control than ever before. In the election nationalists won 300 seats, with the unionists taking 83.

Adapted from Diarmaid Ferriter *The Transformation of Ireland, 1900–2000* published in 2004

Question

Why, according to Diarmaid Ferriter, was the Local Government (Ireland) Act such an important innovation?

Wyndham Land Act, 1903

Perhaps the highpoint of 'Constructive Unionism' was the passing of the Land Act in 1903, initiated by George Wyndham, Chief Secretary of Ireland from 1900 to 1905. In September 1902, landlord Captain John Shawe-Taylor proposed a solution to the land question.

Source X

For the past two hundred years the land war has raged fiercely and continuously, bearing in its train stagnation of trade, paralysis of commercial business and enterprise, and producing hatred and bitterness between various sections and classes of the community. I do not believe there is an Irishman, whatever his political feeling, creed or position, who does not yearn to see a true settlement of the present chaotic, disastrous and ruinous struggle. In the best interests of Ireland I beg most earnestly to invite [names given] to a conference to be held in Dublin within one month of this date.

From an open letter to Irish newspapers from
Captain John Shawe-Taylor, 1902

The Irish Land Conference met December 1902 and its report formed the basis of the Land Act of 1903. The Act was to be ground breaking in a number of ways:

- The Act followed the idea of voluntary land purchase. What was different was the amount of money made available; £12 million in bonuses to landlords to encourage them to sell.

- Tenants were to pay for the land in annual payments over 68 years at 3.25 per cent interest and at a rate guaranteed to be less than rental payments.

- The weaknesses of the Act were that it did little for the landless labourer and landlords were not compelled to sell. The element of compulsion was introduced by the 1909 Land Act.

What was the reaction of the nationalists?

The nationalists were divided in their response to the Wyndham Land Act.

One of the participants in the Irish Land Conference was one of Parnell's closest supporters, William O'Brien. He was to leave the Irish Party to follow a policy of 'conference, conciliation and consent'. The danger for the more radical elements within the nationalist movement was that the Land Act threatened to deal with some of the weaknesses of the land question. Politicians including John Redmond and John Dillon took a rather contradictory stance.

1 What are Dillon's fundamental objections to Wyndham's Act?

2 Source Y comes from the diaries of a certain William Blunt. How reliable is this source in telling us about attitudes towards the Land Act?

Source Y

[Dillon] spoke last night in support of the [Wyndham's] bill. However, he tells me in private that if it wasn't for loyalty to the party, he would be inclined to argue against it in committee and vote against it on the third reading. Dillon's view is that it is useless to get the landlord class on the side of nationalism, that they would always betray it when the pinch came. He thinks that the land trouble is a weapon in nationalist hands, and that to settle the land issue finally would be a risk to home rule.

Adapted from William Blunt, *My Diaries* written on 5 May 1903.
Blunt was a close friend of John Dillon.

How did 'Constructive Unionism' end?

There were two main reasons why 'Constructive Unionism' came to an end, one quite straightforward, the other more complex.

- On the one hand it ended because the Conservative government led by Arthur Balfour resigned in late 1905 to be defeated in a General Election by the Liberal Party led by Henry Campbell-Bannerman.
- The more complex reason is that it was undermined by a loose and unholy alliance of nationalists led by John Dillon and Ulster Unionists.

In 1904 the Land Convention re-formed under the title of the Irish Reform Association. The Association was soon under attack from nationalist and unionist because of discussions about possible devolution and the creation of an Irish council. Such ideas had been put forward by unionist Joseph Chamberlain in the 1880s as an alternative to Home Rule. This time unionists ferociously attacked Wyndham, suspecting that he, his Under-Secretary Sir Anthony MacDonald and Chairman of the Land Convention, Lord Dunraven were behind the scheme. Wyndham resigned in March 1905. The affair had acted to strengthen the hardline nationalist and unionist positions. Another important consequence was the emergence of Ulster Unionism, distinct from unionist sentiment in the south of Ireland or in the rest of the United Kingdom. On 3 March 1905 the Ulster Unionist Council was established.

Source Z

That an Ulster Unionist Council be formed, and that its objects shall be to form an Ulster union for bringing into line all local Unionist associations in the Province of Ulster with a view to consistent and continuous political action, to act as a further connecting link between Ulster Unionists and their parliamentary representatives; to settle in consultation with them the parliamentary policy, and to be the medium of expressing Ulster Unionist opinion as current events may from time to time require, and generally to advance and defend the interests of Ulster Unionism in the Unionist Party.

A resolution passed at a preliminary meeting of the Ulster Unionist Council,
Belfast, 2 December 1904

Question

What were the successes and limitations of 'Constructive Unionism'?

Unit summary

What have you learned in this unit?

You have learned about the failure of Gladstone's Liberal Party to introduce Home Rule as its solution to the Irish Question. The unit has also explained how Home Rule divided the Liberal Party. At the heart of this unit was an analysis of the leadership of Charles Stewart Parnell.

What skills have you used in this unit?

You will have understood that contemporary opinions about issues including Home Rule and Constructive Unionism varied considerably and that evaluation of source material can lead to an adavanced understanding of these different opinions. In this unit you have been asked to work with a number of pictoral sources, you should have a clearer idea of how this type of source can provide the historian with evidence about attitudes towards individuals such as Charles Stewart Parnell and the main issues of the day.

Exam style question

This is the sort of question you will find appearing on the examination paper as a (b) question.

Use Sources W and Y and your own knowledge.

Do you agree with the view that the most significant aspect of 'Constructive Unionism' was land reform?

You tackled a (b) style question at the end of Unit 2. Look back at the exam tips you were given there. Now is the time to build on and develop those tips. What do you have to do to write a successful answer to a (b) question?

Exam tips

- Set up a spider diagram and, in the middle of the spider explain and give examples of political reform.
- Read Sources W and Y carefully. Establish points that **support** and **challenge** the view and set those as spider 'legs'.
- **Think** about appropriate **knowledge** and add a note of this to the different spider 'legs', using knowledge to both **reinforce** and **challenge**.

You are now ready to write up your answer.

Remember to:

- combine the different points into arguments for and against the stated view;
- evaluate the conflicting arguments by reference to the quality of the evidence used;
- reach a supported judgement.

SKILLS BUILDER

1 Using all of the sources and your own knowledge, in what ways did the government's attitude towards Irish affairs change between 1850 and 1905?

2 Set up a debate 'This House believes the Parnell should ultimately be judged a failure.' Remember to use arguments from the time (for and against) when you make out your case.

3 Back to the start: why did the Home Rule fail between 1886 and 1905 and what was the impact of its failure?

RESEARCH TOPIC

Queen Victoria in Dublin, 1900

In 1900 Queen Victoria visited Dublin. As it turned out, this was the year before her death. She received a tremendous welcome. See if you can find out anything about her visit using books or the Internet. You might need to look for the following:

- photographic evidence;

- an itinerary of her visit;

- evidence of how well she was received.

Third Home Rule Bill and Unionism, 1905–14

What is this unit about?

This unit focuses on the growing polarisation of Irish politics over the issue of Home Rule. You will look in detail at Unionism and how it changes over the period in question. The unit will explain the growing militancy. In this unit you will use source material to develop an understanding of Unionism and the nature of evidence.

Key questions

- What was the Third Home Rule Bill crisis?
- How does Unionism change over the period in question?
- What was the significance of individuals including Edward Carson and Andrew Bonar Law?

Historical health warning!

This unit, and the one that follows it, cover roughly the same time period, but in different ways. This unit focuses mainly, although not exclusively, on Unionism in the years running up to the First World War and the constitutional crisis surrounding the Third Home Rule Bill. There are a number of references in this unit to the part played by nationalist groups in the process, most noticeably the Irish Parliamentary Party. Unit 6 addresses the development of the nationalist cause over the same period and then into the war. They have been separated out for reasons of clarity, but you will need to cross-reference between the two units in order to gain the fullest understanding of the dynamics of the period.

Timeline

1905	Ulster Unionist Council set up
1906	Liberal victory in General Election
1907	
January	Augustine Birrell appointed as Chief Secretary for Ireland
May	Irish Party Conference rejects Irish Council Bill
1908	Irish Universities Act passed
1909	
November	House of Lords rejects people's budget
December	Land Act passed
1910	
January	Liberals retain power at General Election
February	Edward Carson chosen as leader of the Irish Unionist Parliamentary Party
December	Liberals retain power at General Election

1911

August	Parliament Act removes Lords veto
September	Ulster Unionist demonstration at Craigavon

1912

April	Introduction of Third Home Rule Bill
July	Andrew Bonar Law's Blenheim Palace speech
September	Signing of Solemn League and Covenant

1913

January	Formation of the Ulster Volunteer Force
November	Formation of the Irish Volunteers

1914

March	Curragh Incident
June	Home Rule Bill proposes exclusion through county option in Ulster
July	Buckingham Palace Conference fails to reach agreement on Home Rule
August	Outbreak of war
September	Home Rule becomes law but is suspended

Definition

Orangeism

The Orange Order was founded in 1795 to defend Protestantism in Ireland. For the first half of the nineteenth century it was identified with rowdy and violent behaviour. The Order gained a very broad popular basis from the 1880s in rejection of the Land League and then Home Rule.

SKILLS BUILDER

Using the extract from Alvin Jackson's book, you are to extract points which, together, will provide you with a clear definition of the term. You may wish to put your points onto a spider chart. Then answer this question:

- What is Unionism?

What was Unionism?

This book so far has mentioned Unionism on a number of occasions. A fair proportion of this unit is devoted to explaining the actions and arguments of unionists at the start of the century. Therefore, it is worth us spending some time trying to work out what Unionism actually was. Below is an extract from a book by Alvin Jackson, who is a Professor of Modern Irish History at Queen's University in Belfast. In this extract, Professor Jackson is defining Unionism as it developed in the nineteenth century.

Source A

Through much of the nineteenth century Unionism – defined very broadly as a belief in the constitutional connection between Britain and Ireland – was the normative [normal] condition in Irish politics.

Even when the definition is tightened and Unionism is seen in a more conventional light (as the movement upholding the Act of Union), its ideological grip upon a wide and diverse section of Irish society, whether northern or southern, was still astonishing. Unionism linked southern landed capital with the world of the northern Presbyterian middle classes; it bound commercial magnates with northern labourers. Unionism commanded a working class constituency in late Victorian Dublin no less than in Belfast.

Defined in institutional terms, Unionism was essentially an amalgam of Irish Toryism, **Orangeism** and the Church of Ireland. The strength of Unionism, certainly in terms of money and social influence, lay in the consensus between landlordism and northern commerce.

From Alvin Jackson *Ireland 1798–1988* published in 1999

How was Unionism transformed?

The period saw a growing divergence between the aspirations of unionists in the south of Ireland and those in the Ulster.

At the end of the last unit, we saw the creation of the Ulster Unionist Council in 1905. This council emerged from a strong unionist tradition that had been revitalised by the attempted introduction of Home Rule in the 1880s. The first leader of the Irish Unionist Parliamentary Party (founded in the year of the First Home Rule Bill in 1886) was Colonel Edward Saunderson. Coming from landowning stock, Saunderson represented the dominance of landowners in the unionist movement. He was successful in combatting Home Rule and attempted to limit the 'Constructive Unionism' of Balfour and Wyndham. The era of Wyndham's reforms (see pages 79–80) fully stretched the relationship between unionist and the Conservative party.

Saunderson was succeeded as head of the unionist movement by Walter Long. In 1906 Long became chair of the Unionist group in Parliament and the Irish Unionist Alliance. The following year he was elected chair of the Ulster Unionist Council. This meant that Long was in charge of the two main strands of Irish Unionism; Ulster and southern based. In January 1910, Long handed over control of Irish Unionism to Carson. Before he did, he defined his understanding of main unionist issues as he understood them.

Source B

Four years ago the government, the party who were then seeking office, declared that Home Rule was to be no part of their programme. They now told them that home rule was to be a leading plan in their programme. They were bound to try and find a reason for that extraordinary change, and he thought it could be found in the fact that at the last general election they [the Liberals] believed that home rule might injure their cause in England, whereas now they thought that possibly they might gain a few votes in Parliament and out of it by adopting the cause of Home Rule. . . . So far as Great Britain was concerned the situation was unchanged; so far as Ireland was concerned the situation was changed but in a direction which pointed in the other direction to home rule. The Unionist Party in Ireland was united, confident and strong . . . Home Rule for Ireland would mean the loss of individual liberty, the absolute insecurity of property, and the negation of everything they cared for affecting the welfare of the country.

The Times newspaper of 5 January 1910 reporting a speech by Walter Long to an Ulster Unionist Council meeting in Belfast

Question

What are Walter Long's arguments against Home Rule?

What pulled Unionism apart?

In his speech in 1910, Walter Long gives the distinct impression that Irish Unionism was united. However, there were a number of reasons why, by 1910, that was no longer the case. From 1900 onwards, the unionist cause

Definition

Trinity College

Trinity College in Dublin was founded in 1592 by Queen Elizabeth. Throughout the eighteenth century, it acted as part of the Protestant Ascendancy but Catholics were admitted in 1793. Trinity College remained an important part of Protestant culture throughout the nineteenth and early twentieth centuries.

fragments and Unionism becomes increasingly defined by and identified with Ulster. Here are some of the reasons why that happened:

- **Southern Unionism** Throughout the nineteenth century there was a strong tradition in Dublin of Unionism, from the academics of **Trinity College** through to a thriving working class unionist tradition. Outside Dublin there were pockets of Unionism beyond the gates of the local squire's house, in areas such as West Cork and County Offaly. However, southern Unionism was weakened by the emergence of a wider electorate (especially after 1884) which meant that, as votes were increasingly cast on sectarian lines, so the number of unionist MPs in southern Ireland diminished. Southern Unionism was, to an extent, undermined by the rise of mass politics. Most of the new voters were Catholics and likely to support Home Rule.

- **Decline of landlordism** The changes in landholding due to successive land reforms (such as the 1870 or 1881 Land Acts) meant the decline in the standing and influence of the unionist landowning class in Ireland. Some land was sold by landlords and bought by tenants.

- **Realignment of northern Unionists** Just as southern Unionism was weakened by the emergence of mass politics, so northern Unionism was strengthened by it. In the early 1900s, a number of individuals and groups emerged to challenge the narrow, landlord led, parliamentary based leadership of Unionism. Foremost among the 'popular unionists' was Tom Sloan, who represented South Belfast as an Independent Unionist MP between 1902 and 1910. The old unionist hierarchy was also shaken by the campaigning of maverick T.W. Russell, who won popular support in the first years of the twentieth century for his campaign for compulsory land purchase to be a central part of land reform. Indeed, Russell's movement captured two seats, East Down and North Fermanagh, from the unionists in 1902–03. Such challenges led to a realignment of Ulster politics and the creation of the Ulster Unionist Council (UUC) in 1905. Although the Council maintained strong links with southern unionists, this was an important point in the long-term development of Unionism.

What was the impact of the Liberal return to power in 1906?

The Conservative government, led by Arthur Balfour, resigned in December 1905. In the election that followed in January 1906 the Liberals won a landslide with 400 seats as opposed to the 133 Conservatives and 24 Liberal Unionists. Mr Long was correct in his assertion that the Liberals had not fought the election on the issue of Ireland; indeed Ireland had not been a burning issue in the election campaign although eighty-three Irish Nationalist MPs were re-elected from Irish constituencies. The priority for the new government was social reform and how to deal with an obstructionist House of Lords. The new Prime Minister, Henry Campbell Bannerman, promised a 'step-by-step' approach.

The gradualist approach was associated with the period in office served by Augustine Birrell. Below are details of three initiatives taken:

Irish Council Bill 1907

The Liberal Prime Minister and Birrell decided to propose some measure of devolution by transferring some of the administrative powers from **Dublin Castle** to a party elected council. However, Birrell played his cards badly, and the Irish Party attacked the Bill as being too limited in its scope. At the meeting to discuss the proposals, nicknamed the 'Convention of Misunderstandings', one of the groups which stood hard against the Bill was the Catholic organisation, the Ancient Order of Hibernians. We will find out more about them in Unit 6 (see pages 105–29). The Bill was withdrawn after being so bitterly condemned at the Convention.

Irish Universities Act 1908

The 'Constructive Unionists' had failed to address the issue of state funded Catholic higher education because of the sensitivity of the Conservative backbenchers to such an idea. Birrell managed to satisfy all vested interests:

- A National University was created with the amalgamation of University College, Galway; University College, Cork; and University College, Dublin. While technically non-denominational, the purpose of the new university was to provide education for Catholics.
- The Protestant Trinity College Dublin was protected and the Presbyterian Queen's College Belfast was made into a full university.

Land Act 1909

The 1903 Land Act had been based on the principle of voluntary agreement between landlord and tenant. The 1909 Act introduced the idea of compulsory purchase in some of the more over-populated regions of the country. However, the act slightly reduced the incentive for the landlord to sell his land and the tenant to buy.

What were the significance of the 1910 Elections and the 1911 Parliament Act?

In 1909 the Liberal Chancellor of the Exchequer, David Lloyd George presented his so-called 'People Budget' to Parliament. Included in the budget were proposals that would, in Lloyd George's words, hit the rich. These included an increase in income tax, a supertax for the very wealthy and a land tax based on surveys of land ownership. The budget passed through the House of Commons but was rejected by the House of Lords. In response Asquith called a General Election promising Home Rule in the

Definition

Dublin Castle

The castle was the administrative heart of British rule in Ireland. It was where the Chief Secretary and civil service were based.

Question

How radical were these reforms and how different were they from the reforms of 'Constructive Unionism'?

election campaign to maximise the support of the Irish in England. In the General Election of January 1910, the handsome Liberal majority of 1906 was slashed to only two seats. The initiative was back with the Irish Party and fellow nationalists who, with eighty-two seats between them, held the balance of power. The failure to resolve the constitutional struggle between Commons and Lords resulted in a second General Election in 1910, this one in December. The main election issue of was whether the Lords had the right to veto Commons legislation or whether it just had the right to delay it. The December 1910 election resulted in another Liberal victory over the Conservatives, this time by one seat.

The significance of the 1911 Parliament Act is that it removed the Lords veto. If a Bill was passed by the House of Commons in three successive sessions within a two-year time span, on the third occasion it would become law with or without the consent of the House of Lords. This removed a potentially very significant obstacle to the passage of Irish Home Rule. The leader of the Irish Party, John Redmond, had a good working relationship with Ireland's Chief Secretary Augustine Birrell. In 1911 and early 1912 Birrell was still the most important influence in government circles over Irish policy. In 1911 it seemed as if the Irish nationalists were in a position to call the shots. In April 1912 Asquith introduced the Third Home Rule Bill in the House of Commons. Below is a postcard from 1911–12. It shows John Redmond supposedly leading Liberal leaders Asquith, Lloyd George and Winston Churchill.

Source C

5.1 *Their Irish Master*, postcard, 1911/12.

Biography

Edward Carson (1854–1935)

Edward Carson was born into a Church of Ireland family in Dublin in 1854. He was educated at Trinity College, Dublin before entering the legal profession. In 1892 he was appointed Solicitor-general for Ireland before moving to England to practise his profession. In 1892 he became a Unionist MP for Trinity College. In 1910 he became leader of the Irish Unionists at Westminster, all MPs except himself and the MP for South County Dublin representing Ulster constituencies. Carson was an energetic defender of Ulster's interests and a fierce opponent of Home Rule. In 1914 he pledged the Ulster Volunteer Force for service overseas and after the 1916 Rising, he offered their services again 'for the maintenance of the King's authority'. Carson joined the Cabinet in July but resigned in 1918. In 1921 he resigned as leader of the Unionists after Partition had been secured. Carson died in 1935.

What was proposed by the Home Rule Bill of 1912?

The Third Home Rule Bill was very similar to the Second Home Rule Bill in its proposals. The main features were:

- There would be a two chamber Irish Assembly with forty members of the Senate and 164 members of the lower House.

- There would continue to be Irish representation at Westminster with forty-two Irish MPs sitting in the Imperial Parliament.

- The Irish Assembly could impose new taxes and could vary imperial taxes.

- A Lord Lieutenant would replace the administrative powers of Dublin Castle.

The introduction of the Irish Home Rule Bill in Parliament brought bitter opposition from the leader of the Conservative Party, Andrew Bonar Law. The debate was held both inside and outside Parliament.

What was the Blenheim Palace speech?

The tension surrounding Home Rule throughout July was considerable. The Prime Minister, Asquith, visited Dublin on 19 July and received a tremendous reception. In the evening, Asquith spoke at a meeting at the Theatre Royal, chaired by John Redmond.

Source D

I have come here to Dublin to assure the people of Ireland of the resolute determination of the British government, the British House of Commons and the British people to bring your great cause to a speedy and triumphant issue. [The unionist campaign] is purely destructive in its objects, anarchic and chaotic in its methods . . . Ireland is a nation, not two nations, but one nation.

Herbert Asquith speaking in Dublin, 19 July 1912

The response of the Unionists was to arrange for the Conservative Party leader, Andrew Bonar Law, to address a crowd of around 13,000 at Blenheim Palace, ancestral seat of the Duke of Marlborough, family home to Lord Randolph Churchill and birthplace of his son Winston who was Asquith's First Lord of the Admiralty.

Source E

5.2 Andrew Bonar Law arriving at Blenheim Palace, 27 July 1912.

Source F

[The Prime Minister] has returned from Ireland and he has told us that the Parliament Bill was not carried for nothing. It was to force through Parliament the Home Rule proposals which at the election were carefully hidden from the people of this country – proposals which they are trying to carry, not only without the consent, but as we know, and as they know, against the will of the people.

The Chief Liberal Whip has told us also that the Home Rule Bill will be carried through the House of Commons before Christmas. Perhaps it will . . . I do not know. But I do know this – that we do not acknowledge their right to carry such a revolution by such means. In our opposition to them . . . we shall not be guided by the considerations or bound by the restraints which would influence us in an ordinary constitutional struggle.

While I had still in the party a position of less responsibility than that which I have now, I said that in my opinion if an attempt were made, without the clearly expressed will of the people of this country, and as part of a corrupt parliamentary bargain, to deprive these men of their birthright, they would be justified in resisting by all means in their power, including force. I said so then, and I say so now, with a full sense of the responsibility which attaches to my position, that if the attempt be made under present conditions, I can imagine no length of resistance to which Ulster will go, in which I shall not be ready to support them, and in which they will not be supported by the overwhelming majority of the British people.

Andrew Bonar Law's speech at Blenheim Palace as reported by *The Times*, 29 July 1912

SKILLS BUILDER

You teacher will want to decide whether you work in groups or on your own for this activity.

- You need to identify the main points of this speech.
- You then need to consider why Andrew Bonar Law's speech was considered to be controversial.
- The historian George Dangerfield called Bonar Law's speech *'a crude step into rebellion'*. Was he right to do so?

What was Ulster Day, 1912?

As the Home Rule Bill made its way through the House of Commons, the Ulster Unionists made plans for a show of political strength and solidarity which would, hopefully, force the Liberal government's hand. Gestures, images and symbols became all important in the debate over Home Rule. They drew up a Solemn League and Covenant, outlining their position regarding Home Rule in clear and unambiguous language. Carson was the first to sign the Solemn League and Covenant on 28 September 1912, using a silver pen given to him the night before. Carson was also presented with a silk banner, said to have belonged to troops of King William in 1690. After Carson had signed the Covenant and the photographs had been taken, 450,000 men and women signed the Covenant. It was a powerful message to Asquith's government.

Source G

5.3 Edward Carson signs the Solemn League and Covenant, 28 September 1912.

Source H

Being convinced in our consciences that Home Rule would be disastrous to the material well-being of Ulster, as well as of the whole of Ireland, subversive to our civil and religious freedom, destructive of our citizenship, and perilous to the unity of the Empire, we, whose names are underwritten, men of Ulster, loyal subjects of his Gracious Majesty King George V, humbly relying on the God whom our fathers in the days of stress and trial confidently trusted, do hereby pledge ourselves in solemn covenant throughout this our time of threatened calamity to stand by one another in defending for ourselves and our children our cherished position of equal citizenship in the United Kingdom and in using all means which may be found necessary to defeat the present conspiracy to set up a home rule parliament in Ireland. And in the event of such a Parliament being forced upon us we further and mutually pledge ourselves to refuse to recognise its authority. In sure confidence that God will defend the right, we hereto subscribe our names. God Save the King.

The Solemn League and Covenant, 1912

SKILLS BUILDER

What are the issues covered by the Solemn League and Covenant?

Kipling's Ulster

The Ulster Unionists had strong support among the more patriotic elements of British society. The most famous literary supporter of Empire was Rudyard Kipling. In his poem *Ulster, 1912*, Kipling expresses his view of Home Rule.

Source I

1. THE DARK eleventh hour
Draws on and sees us sold
To every evil power
We fought against of old.
Rebellion, rapine, hate,
Oppression, wrong and greed
Are loosed to rule our fate,
By England's act and deed.

2. The Faith in which we stand,
The laws we made and guard,
Our honour, lives, and land
Are given for reward
To Murder done by night,
To Treason taught by day,
To folly, sloth, and spite,
And we are thrust away.

3. The blood our fathers spilt,
Our love, our toils, our pains,
Are counted us for guilt,
And only bind our chains.
Before an Empire's eyes
The traitor claims his price.
What need of further lies?
We are the sacrifice.

4. We asked no more than leave
To reap where we had sown,
Through good and ill to cleave
To our own flag and throne.
Now England's shot and steel
Beneath that flag must show
How loyal hearts should kneel
To England's oldest foe.

5. We know the war prepared
On every peaceful home,
We know the hells declared
For such as serve not Rome—
The terror, threats, and dread
In market, hearth, and field—
We know, when all is said,
We perish if we yield.

6. Believe, we dare not boast,
Believe, we do not fear
We stand to pay the cost
In all that men hold dear.
What answer from the North?
One Law, one Land, one Throne
If England drive us forth
We shall not fall alone!

From Rudyard Kipling's poem called 'Ulster' written in 1912

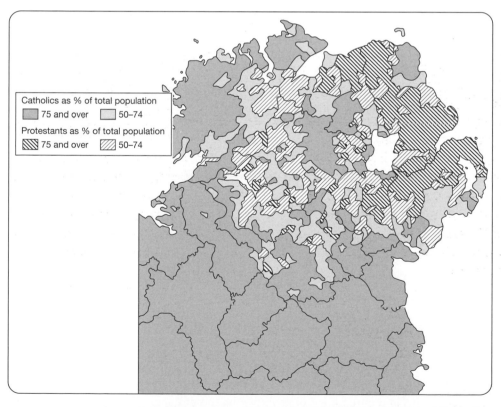

5.4 Map showing the distribution of Protestants and Catholics in Northern Ireland in 1911.

Catholics as % of total population
- 75 and over
- 50–74

Protestants as % of total population
- 75 and over
- 50–74

SKILLS BUILDER

Even though Kipling was not directly involved with the Home Rule crisis, is this poem useful to an historian in their investigation of the Home Rule issue of 1912 to 1914?

Partition

The idea of Partition had been mooted in Liberal circles in August 1911 as a four county solution: Down, Londonderry, Antrim and Armagh. The counties of Ulster had strong unionist majorities. The idea was brought to the Cabinet as a possible solution by Winston Churchill and David Lloyd George in February 1912. The Cabinet decided against proceeding with the idea of any such compromise solution. This was because neither Asquith nor any of his leading ministers felt it necessary or politically wise at this stage to make such concessions. The Home Rule Bill made no mention of Ulster or any suggestion of two Irelands. In June 1912, a Cornish Liberal MP, T.G. Agar Robartes, tabled an amendment to the Home Rule Bill suggesting a four county opt-out. This was perhaps a golden opportunity for the leadership of the Liberal party to accept such a compromise as a means of resolving the issue but they failed to take the opportunity and the amendment was defeated. The Bill was finally passed by the House of Commons in January 1913 but rejected by the House of Lords.

The events of 1912 and the summer of 1913 focused the minds of leading Liberal politicians, including Churchill and Lloyd George, as to what might be the best solution.

Definition

Moratorium

is another word for a delay or temporary suspension.

Question

What is being suggested by Churchill in his letter to Redmond?

Source J

I do not believe there is any real feeling against home rule in the Tory party apart from the Ulster question, but they hate the government, are bitterly desirous of turning it out, and see in the resistance of Ulster an extreme parliamentary force which they will not hesitate to use to the full . . . My general view is that something should be done to afford the characteristically Protestant and Orange counties the option of a **moratorium** of several years before acceding to the Irish Parliament.

A letter from Winston Churchill to John Redmond, 31 August 1913

The discussion about the possibility of a separate solution for Ulster became public in September with the publication in *The Times* newspaper of a letter from leading Liberal peer Lord Loreburn suggesting some form of compromise. In October 1913 Churchill publicly suggested partition for Ulster in a speech in Dundee. The Irish Party leadership made clear their views on such a possibility.

Source K

Irish Nationalists can never be assenting parties to the mutilation of the Irish nation; Ireland is a unit. It is true that within the bosom of a nation there is room for diversities in the treatment of government and of administration, but a unit Ireland is and a unit Ireland must remain . . . The two-nation theory is to us an abomination and a blasphemy . . .

John Redmond in a speech to Irish Nationalists in Limerick, 12 October 1913

Whatever Redmond's statements, by this point the initiative had passed to those in government such as Lloyd George who favoured some form of partition. By March 1914, the government were proposing a county by county opt-out system and a delay of six years in bringing opted-out counties under any form of Home Rule. Although in public Carson claimed that he would not accept such a compromise (in the House of Commons in March 1914 he called it a 'sentence of death with a stay of execution for six years'), in private he had come a long way. By this time both Carson and the leadership of Ulster Unionists had come to the conclusion that the best way ahead was permanent exclusion of six counties of Ulster that contained a Unionist and Protestant majority: Antrim, Armagh, Down, Fermanagh, Londonderry/Derry and Tyrone. In May 1914, the Home Rule Bill that passed through the House of Commons proposed for a county based exclusion for six years. The House of Lords amended the exclusion clause to the nine counties of Ulster for ever. A conference was called for July to meet at Buckingham Palace to resolve the issues. The following source is from a record of the conference and clearly highlights the extent of the disagreement.

SKILLS BUILDER

Using Source L and your own knowledge, what were the main points of disagreement between Unionist and Nationalist in the summer of 1914?

Source L

The Prime Minister indicated that, in his opinion, the two serious outstanding points were the areas of exclusion and the time limit.

Sir Edward Carson then made a strong appeal to Mr Redmond and Mr Dillon to consent to the total exclusion of [nine county] Ulster in the interests of the earliest possible unity of Ireland. He argued that if a smaller area were excluded, the reunion of the whole of Ireland would be delayed. Mr Redmond indicated that it would be quite impossible for him, under any circumstances, to agree.

Mr Redmond then read the following memorandum: The Irish National Party have all along been, and still are, strongly of the opinion that no satisfactory settlement of the Irish question can be obtained by the exclusion of any portion of Ireland from the operation of the Home Rule Bill. The Irish Party only consented to negotiate on the basis of exclusion because the leaders of the Ulster Unionists repeatedly and emphatically refused to consider any other proposal.

Having examined carefully all other possible methods, the National Party came to the conclusion that the only practical method was by giving each county an option to exclude itself by ballot from the operation of the Act. . . . Sir Edward Carson, Lord Lansdowne and Mr Bonar Law declared that upon the basis of county option no agreement was possible.

Minutes from the Buckingham Palace Conference, July 1914

The outcome of the Buckingham Palace meeting was indecisive. That no deal was made and nothing finalised reflects the deep disagreement and the entrenched positions taken by either side. The constitutional debate had also, to a certain extent, been overtaken by extra parliamentary action as we shall see in the next section.

Definition

Paramilitary

A paramilitary force is an unofficial military organisation.

What was the Ulster Volunteer Force?

The constitutional discussions about Home Rule and partition took place against the backdrop of the growth of **paramilitary** organisations on both sides.

Throughout 1911, unionists had been buying arms and participating in military drill. Twice in a year, demonstrations of military drill and efficiency were put on at the home of Captain James Craig at Craigavon. In January 1913, the Ulster Unionist Council decided to formalise such activity by creating a paramilitary organisation, the Ulster Volunteer Force (UVF). Throughout 1913, the UVF attracted recruits, drilled and trained. Many within the Orange Order and sympathisers in Britain gave substantial amounts of money for the organisation of the UVF and the purchase of arms, uniforms, transport vehicles and ambulances. They were supplied with imported weapons, despite a government ban on importing weapons issued in December 1913. By the summer 1914, the UVF had anything up to 100,000 members and it flexed its military muscle as the tension over Home Rule mounted.

On the night of 24–25 April, the UVF staged an extraordinary event. Around 3 million rounds of ammunition and 25,000 rifles were landed at Larne and other Ulster seaside towns including Donaghadee. The army and police did nothing to prevent the unloading of such a large amount of arms despite the fact that it was illegal. Larne was a propaganda success for the UVF. It also limited the negotiating flexibility of the Unionist leadership, now hemmed in on one side by a well armed paramilitary force. From now on it would be impossible for the Unionist leadership to consider any compromise in discussions with the government over Ulster's future.

SKILLS BUILDER

What impression is given by this postcard?

How useful is this postcard to an historian investigating the 1914 gun running incident?

Source M

Historic Events]   **WAITING FOR THE GUNS AT BANGOR, 24th APRIL, 1914.**   [Series

5.5 Postcard showing UVF members waiting to land munitions, April 1914.

Source N

[The army shall not] be used in Ulster to prevent or interfere with any step which may thereafter be taken in Ulster to organise resistance to the enforcement of [the Home Rule] Act in Ulster nor to suppress any such resistance there unless and until the present Parliament shall have been dissolved and a period of three months shall have lapsed after the meeting of a new Parliament.

Resolution of the Shadow Cabinet, 4 February 1914

Question

What is the implication of the resolution taken in Source N?

What was the Curragh mutiny?

The tension in Ulster and Unionist mistrust had been made much worse by government bungling in March of 1914. A number of senior army officers including Field Marshal Frederick Roberts and Director of Military Operations at the War Office, General Henry Wilson had expressed concerns about the possibility of the British Army being used in Ulster to enforce Home Rule. Their concerns were picked up by the leader of the Conservative Party, Andrew Bonar Law. He agreed to put to the Shadow Cabinet a proposal to amend the Annual Army Act if the government went ahead with Home Rule without calling an election.

The stance taken by the Conservative Party did not help to diffuse tension, nor did the actions of the Government that followed. In March 1914, the Secretary of State for War John Seeley decided to deploy more British Army troops in Ulster to safeguard weapons dumps. He also informed the Commander-in-Chief in Ireland, Sir Arthur Paget, that any soldier who wished to make himself absent from duty in Ulster could do so. However, those who stayed on and then refused to obey orders would be dismissed. The message was clumsily passed on to the soldiers based at the Curragh Camp in County Kildare. The following pieces of evidence are letters from soldiers serving at the Curragh base:

Source O

At 11 o'clock this morning the Colonel called a conference of all soldiers and put forward the following question: 'If the regiment is ordered to take action against Ulster in the interests of the preservation of peace, are you prepared to go or do you wish to resign your commission? If you resign your commission, you will be dismissed from the service without a pension.

We all loathed the idea of going to Ulster for the sake of a few dirty Nationalists who loathe the army and who are most unloyal to anything to do with Britain. You cannot imagine a more trying day, when in a matter of an hour or so we had to decide between 'shooting down Loyalists and starting a fresh job on nothing'.

From Second Lieutenant E.G. Miles to his father,
21 March 1914

Source P

You have probably heard by now full details of the trouble here, but some notes direct may interest you. Who is exactly responsible I know not, but we are pretty well agreed that the crisis was not due to political passion but to an absurd want of tact. 48 hours ago the Grand Military and the like were the sole topic of conversation – all are sick to death of the subject of 'home rule' and for weeks I've never heard it mentioned in the mess or hunting field.

Then suddenly a bolt from the blue – officers all summoned and told that they must within two hours undertake to fight against Ulster to the end, or resign, and that resign meant dismissal. 5th and 16th Lancers resigned in a body at once.

The next morning down came 'A.P.' [Arthur Paget] himself and in half an hour succeeded in wholly upsetting the applecart again. . . . I think that had this affair not arisen it is just possible that the troops might have drifted into active operations against the Ulstermen: but that is out of the question now. If we do anything at all it must clearly be for 'law and order' and nothing else. I suppose that I'm as moderate and impartial as anyone here, for in principle I'm a home ruler and not swept away by Ulster heroics.

Major P. Howell, Curragh Camp,
writing a letter to a friend, 22 March 1914

SKILLS BUILDER

Sources O and P are letters from March 1914 written by army officers serving at the Curragh Camp. How useful are such letters to an historian who is researching the events of the Curragh Mutiny?

The Curragh Mutiny was a public relations disaster for the government. In the end, 58 cavalry officers refused to participate in any offensive operations in Ulster. The mutiny gave the impression that the government would not be able to rely on the army to enforce Home Rule in Ulster if violence broke out. In the wake of the Curragh mutiny, General Sir Hubert Gough was able to gain assurances from the Asquith's government that they would not use force against the Ulster Unionists. The episode seemed to support nationalists' suspicions that the army was prejudiced against them and the unionist suspicions that the government had planned to use the army to force Home Rule on them. The result was a further polarising of positions.

What was the nationalist response to the UVF?

The response of the nationalists to the creation and activities of the Ulster Volunteer Force was mixed. Some, with a distorted logic welcomed it because it was a challenge to the British government as much as a threat to themselves. The eventual leader of the 1916 Easter Rising, Patrick Pearse, welcomed the foundation of the UVF. The *Irish Freedom* was a nationalist newspaper.

A more concrete response came from Eoin MacNeill, a history professor at University College Dublin.

Source Q

Negotiations with the Orangemen might be opened on these lines: You are creating a Provisional Government of Ulster – make it a Provisional Government of Ireland and we will recognise and obey it. . . . Hitherto England has governed Ireland through the Orange Lodges, now she proposes to govern Ireland through the **AOH**. You object; so do we. Why not unite and get rid of the English? They are the real difficulty; their presence here the real incongruity.

From an article written by Patrick Pearse in the journal *Irish Freedom*, 1914

Definition

AOH

AOH stands for the Ancient Order of Hibernians. It was set up in 1836 in the United States of America to protect the interests of Catholics. In Ireland, the AOH became strongly linked to the Irish Party, hence Pearse's comments.

Source R

The Ulster Volunteer movement is essentially and obviously a home rule movement. It claims, no doubt, to hold Ireland 'for the Empire'; but really it is no matter whether Ireland is to be held for the Empire or for the Empyrean [heaven], against the Pope, against John Redmond, against the man in the moon. What matters is by whom Ireland is to be held.

The true meaning of this extraordinary development is dawning painfully on English Unionists. They are beginning to understand that Sir Edward Carson has knocked the bottom out of Unionism . . . in any case it appears that the British Army cannot now be used to prevent the enrolment, drilling and reviewing of Volunteers in Ireland.

It is evident that the only solution now possible is for the Empire either to make terms with Ireland or to let Ireland go her own way. In any case, it is manifest [clear] that all Irish people, Unionist as well as nationalist, are determined to have their own way in Ireland. It is not to follow that, and it will not follow, that any part of Ireland, majority or minority, is to interfere with the liberty of any other part. Sir Edward Carson may yet, at the head of his Volunteers, 'march to Cork'. If so, their progress will probably be accompanied by the greetings of ten times their number of National Volunteers, and Cork will give them a hospitable and memorable reception.

Article by Eoin MacNeill in Irish language newspaper *An Claidheamh Soluis*, 1 November 1913

SKILLS BUILDER

1 What are the similarities between Sources Q and R? In answering your question you should consider the following:

- content
- tone
- implication.

2 It can be argued that the authors of both sources are naïve in their assumptions about the Ulster Volunteer Force.

- Are the authors simplistic in their views?
- Does this mean that both sources should be discounted as unreliable?

What were the aims of the Irish Volunteers?

The reaction to MacNeill's article in the nationalist community was considerable. On 25 November 1913, a meeting was held in Dublin at which the Irish Volunteer movement was founded. The response from the Irish Party at this stage was mixed; a number of ordinary members joining the Volunteers but the leadership staying aloof. The aims of the Volunteers at this point were somewhat vague:

- The Volunteers were not formed to put pressure on the British government, especially because at this moment it was attempting to get the Home Rule Bill through Parliament.
- It was not the aim of the Volunteers to combat the UVF. This was despite the fact that MacNeill and other leaders feared that the UVF would be used to harass nationalists in the north of Ireland.
- The aim, therefore, of the Irish Volunteers was to mobilise to defend and protect Ireland.

The creation of the Irish Volunteers without John Redmond's consent revealed his relatively weak position within the nationalist movement by this stage (something that will be explored at greater length in Unit 6). At first the Irish Party condemned the creation of a nationalist paramilitary force. Redmond and his parliamentary colleagues had, for some months, been condemning Carson and the Ulster Volunteer Force. This gave the initiative to the more radical Fenian IRB, which infiltrated the Irish Volunteers at every level. Eventually, in June 1914, Redmond acted to take control of the Irish Volunteers movement by insisting that the ruling Provisional Committee accept twenty-five new members from the Irish Party.

What happened at Howth?

The Irish Volunteers attracted members from across all sections of Irish society. The Catholic Irish gentry signed up to the movement as they had in 1798. By July 1914, the Volunteer force had around 160,000 members and was determined to make a mark. On 16 July, the Volunteers copied the UVF's gun-running by landing 1,500 Mauser guns and 25,000 rounds of ammunition. The army was called out and three unarmed civilians were shot dead by nervous troops in Batchelor's Walk, Dublin. The irony of the fact that the army had not intervened when the UVF had landed weapons at Larne was not lost on the nationalists.

Source S

5.6 Photograph of Irish Volunteers in training, 1914.

SKILLS BUILDER

There are clear strengths and weaknesses for the historian using this photograph as part of an enquiry into the Irish Volunteers. What are they?

Source T

But Asquith's delaying tactics, however dangerous, had logic – even if its subtlety is seldom appreciated. It may well be that Asquith was banking on the likelihood that the Unionists were bluffing; and, even if the Ulstermen defied the odds and moved to act, he could still win the game by forcing them to postpone their 'decisive action' until the parliamentary recess had begun. In these circumstances, certainly in the view of one very senior and experienced Unionist strategist, the Ulster rebellion would have been a fiasco and Asquith could have imposed a politically convenient settlement. Even as it was, some slight but suggestive divisions were beginning to open up within the Ulster Unionist leadership by the end of July 1914, particularly between Carson and Craig.

Adapted from Alvin Jackson's *Home Rule – An Irish History 1800–2000*, published in 2004

Outbreak of war

As the summer of 1914 began to fade, it was clear that there was no agreement about the future of Ulster and Home Rule. The concern was that one or the other side would contemplate using the paramilitary strength it had built up to assert its position. There was, therefore, a possibility of civil war at worst and the likelihood of significant unrest. However, for once, Irish affairs were overshadowed by events of even greater significance. On 4 August 1914, the British Empire declared war on Germany. The Government of Ireland Bill received the royal assent on 18 September 1914 but it was preceded three days before by another Bill postponing the implementation of Home Rule until the end of the Great War. The course of Irish history was about to be changed forever by events in Europe and the wider world. The impact of the First World War is very well summarised by the historian R.F. Foster.

Unit summary

What have you learned in this unit?

The nature of the unionist response to Home Rule changed in the period in question. The commitment of the Liberals to Home Rule remained although it was in part driven by the number of seats held in the House of Commons. The tabling of the Third Home Rule Bill in April 1912 was to provide a watershed. It led to a constitutional crisis of profound significance. The emergence of the compromise of an Ulster exclusion was to further change the nature of Unionism. The constitutional wrangling should be seen against the backdrop of the growth of paramilitary organisations in Ulster. The outbreak of the Great War temporarily defused the Ulster crisis.

What skills have you used in this unit?

Your evaluation of the source material will have helped develop your understanding of the changing nature of the Unionist campaign. You will have assessed the utility of certain different types of evidence as part of an enquiry.

Exam style question

This is the sort of question you will find appearing on the examination paper as a (b) question.

Study Sources L, Q and T and use your own knowledge.

Do you agree with the view, hinted at in Source L, that by the summer of 1914 there were no grounds for compromise over Home Rule?

You have already a tackled a (b) style question. Look back to the exam tips you were given there because you will need to use them in order to answer this question. At the end of Unit 4 you created a spider diagram as a plan. This time, use whichever sort of plan you like best and which works for you. But be sure to plan!

Exam tips

- Be very sure you know what **'view'** is being expressed in Source L.
- **Analyse** and **interpret** Sources Q and T so as to establish points that **support** and **challenge** the view given in Source L.
- **Cross-reference** between the sources by focusing on support and challenge.
- Use your **wider knowledge** both to reinforce and to challenge the points derived from the sources
- Combine the points into **arguments** for and against the view given in Source L.
- **Evaluate** the conflicting arguments by considering the **quality of the evidence** used, involving a consideration of provenance (where appropriate) and the weight of evidence and range of supporting knowledge you can find in support.
- Present a **supported judgement** as to the validity of the stated view and/or any alternatives.

SKILLS BUILDER

1 Go back to Professor Alvin Jackson's definition of Unionism on page 84. How far had Unionism changed by 1914 and why?

2 Form yourselves into discussion groups. You are to answer the following question:

Why did Unionists fear Home Rule?

This is a difficult and complex question that cannot be answered from information in this unit alone. In your discussion groups, you need to come up with at least five points that you should place on a spider chart. You are to prioritise these points in order of importance.

3 Debate time.

Your are to use the information from the last exercise and the work covered so far. You are to present one of the two following arguments:

- The case by Edward Carson against Home Rule.
- The case by John Redmond in favour of Home Rule.

RESEARCH TOPIC

Biography boxes

In the course of this unit, a number of individuals have been mentioned as significant figures. However, the author of the book has not gone into much detail about these characters. Here is your opportunity to find out more about some of these people. This is a suggested list of people:

- Captain James Craig

- Colonel Saunderson

- Tom Sloan

- T.W. Russell.

UNIT

6 Revolutionary nationalism and the Easter Rising, 1900–16

What is this unit about?

This unit focuses on the emergence of revolutionary nationalism and the impact of the First World War. The most significant event covered in this unit is the Easter Rising of 1916. The Rising, led by Patrick Pearse, was a demonstration of the desire among some nationalists to reject the constitutional path of John Redmond and the Irish party. Their alternative was to agitate for a separate state, independent from Britain and without any concession to Unionism.

The Easter Rising was doomed from the start as a military exercise. However, the reactions of the British government to the Rising changed attitudes towards revolutionary nationalism in Ireland and helped create a new political context for the debate about Ireland's future.

Key questions

- How did revolutionary nationalism develop in the years 1900 to 1916?
- What was the significance and immediate impact of the Easter Rising in 1916?

Timeline

1884	Creation of the Gaelic Athletic Association
1893	Gaelic League set-up
1896	Irish Socialist Republican Party founded
1899	*United Irishman* newspaper set up by Arthur Griffith
1900	Foundation of Cumann na nGaedheal by Arthur Griffth
1905	Arthur Griffith proposes creation of Sinn Féin
1909	James Larkin sets up the Irish Transport and General Workers Union (ITGWU)
1913	
August	ITGWU Dublin strike begins
November	Irish Citizen Army created, Irish Volunteers founded by Eoin MacNeill
1914	
April	Foundation of Cumann na mBan
July	Howth gun running incident
August	Britain declares war on Germany
September	Redmond pledging Irish Volunteer support for the war effort at Woodenbridge leads to split

Definition

Cultural revival

This term is used to describe the period towards the end of the nineteenth century when there was a renewed interest in Irish culture from the Irish language to Irish sports. Many groups were founded during this period in order to promote Irish activities, most notably the Gaelic Athletic Association (GAA).

Hurling

This is a game played with sticks called hurleys and a ball. The aim of the game is to hit the ball into a goal for three points or between two posts for one point.

Question

Study Source A. What does Cusack argue are the reasons for promoting Irish sports and pastimes?

1915		
	May	Military Council of IRB set-up
	July	Gaelic League takes a more political line
1916		
	April	German ship *Aud* is intercepted by the Royal Navy, Roger Casement arrested, Rising takes place but is defeated
	May	Leaders of the Rising executed

What was the Gaelic Athletic Association?

Towards the end of the nineteenth century, a number of groups and associations were founded in Ireland that, together, were to represent a **cultural revival** and, in the early part of the twentieth century, a cultural revolution. A central element of this cultural revival was the belief in a return to 'Irish-Ireland'; an Ireland untainted by English rule. Although many of the organisations that were set up as part of this cultural revival were initially non-sectarian, by 1900 many had become more identified with a vision of a Catholic Ireland.

The late nineteenth century saw a growth in interest in Irish culture. Known as the 'cultural revival' it was to have a political as well as cultural impact. The Gaelic Athletic Association was founded in 1884 by Irish civil servant Michael Cusack. His concern was the spread in popularity of so-called 'foreign games' such as rugby, football, hockey and cricket at the expense of Irish games, notably Irish football and **hurling**. The worst thing for Cusack was that all athletics competitions in Ireland were arranged and run by the English Athletics Association. This is an extract from Cusack's letter to *The Irishman* newspaper in 1884 that triggered the meeting in a hotel in Thurles in November of that year at which the GAA was formally set up.

Source A

No movement having for its object the social and political advancement of a nation from the tyranny of imported and enforced customs and manners can be regarded as perfect if it has not made adequate provision for the preservation and cultivation of the National pastimes of the people. Voluntary neglect of such pastimes is a sure sign of National decay and of approaching dissolution.

The strength and energy of a race are largely dependent on the national pastimes for the development of a spirit of courage and endurance. The corrupting influences which, for several years, have been devastating the sporting grounds of our cities and towns are fast spreading to the rural population. Foreign and hostile laws and the pernicious [evil] influence of a hitherto dominant race drove the Irish people from the trysting [meeting] places at the cross-roads and the hurling fields, back to their cabin where, but a few short years before, famine and fever had reigned supreme. In these wretched homes . . . the Irish peasant too often wasted his evenings and his holidays, in smoking and card-playing.

From Michael Cusack 'A Word About Irish Athletics' in *The Irishman*, 11 October 1884

What were the main features of the Gaelic Athletic Association?

Although the GAA attempted to codify Irish sports mirroring the process that had taken place in England, which marked the birth of modern team games sports as we know it, that was the limits of the GAA's association with England. The GAA also took its inspiration from European sport's groups such as the Czech *Soklol* founded in the 1860s to promote a mix of physical well-being and nationalist ideas. Although Cusack initially intended for the GAA to represent all strands within Irish society, that was not to be the case for long. The organisation had strong links with the Catholic Church from the start, Archbishop Croke of Cashel being one of the first patrons. The GAA maintained strong links with the Irish Party of Parnell, but, by 1900 it had strong links to the Irish National Brotherhood. Initial rules that banned participation in so-called 'foreign sports' and the participation of members of the Royal Irish Constabulary were restated in 1901 and 1906, respectively. The GAA was to play a very important role in the development of a new Irish nationalism, which looked ahead to a separation of Ireland and Britain.

SKILLS BUILDER

Why do you think the GAA produced such a poster?

Source B

6.1 A GAA poster explaining some of the different aspects of hurling, from around 1900.

Biography

Douglas Hyde (1860–1949)

Hyde was born into a Protestant family from Roscommon in 1860. He became an academic at Trinity College Dublin and it was from this position that he helped launch the Gaelic League on 1893. Concerned about the increasingly political nature of many of the League's followers, Hyde resigned as President of the Gaelic League in 1915. He was briefly a Senator in the Irish Parliament up to 1925. In 1938 he was chosen as Ireland's first President, a post he held up to 1945.

What was the Gaelic League?

From the 1870s onwards, a number of organisations were set up to promote the awareness and the use of the Irish language. The number speaking the language had declined with the impact of the Famine, migration and English based education. Indeed, the 1891 census revealed that there were only 66,000 out of a population of 4.7 million who spoke Irish alone in the country. In 1876 the Society for the Preservation of the Irish Language was formed, to be followed in 1880 by the Gaelic Union. One of the most successful organisations for the promotion of the Irish language was the Gaelic League founded in 1893 by Eoin MacNeill and inspired and led by Douglas Hyde. The following extract is from Hyde's lecture 'The Necessity for De-Anglicising Ireland' delivered to the Irish National Literary Society in Dublin on 25 November 1892.

Source C

I wish to show you that in Anglicising ourselves wholesale we have thrown away with a light heart the best claim which we have upon the world's recognition of us as a separate nationality.

It has always been very curious to me how Irish sentiment . . . continues to apparently hate the English, and at the same time continues to imitate them . . . It is a fact that although they adopt English habits and copy England in every way, the great bulk of Irishmen and Irishwomen over the whole world are known to be filled with a dull, ever-abiding animosity against her . . . Such movements as Young Irelandism, Fenianism, Land Leagueism, and Parliamentary obstruction seem always to gain their sympathy and support. It is just because there appears no earthly chance of their becoming good members of the Empire that I urge that they should not remain in the anomalous position they are in,

Continued opposite . . .

Source C continued . . .

but since they absolutely refuse to become the one thing, that they become the other; cultivate what they have rejected, and build up an Irish nation on Irish lines.

We must teach ourselves to be less sensitive, we must teach ourselves not to be ashamed of ourselves, because the Gaelic people can never produce its best before the world as long as it remains tied to the apron-strings of another race and another island, waiting for it to move before it will venture to take any step itself.

In conclusion, I would earnestly appeal to every one, whether Unionist or Nationalist, who wishes to see the Irish nation produce its best – surely whatever our politics are we all wish that – to set his face against this constant running to England for our books, literature, music, games, fashions, and ideas. I appeal to every one whatever his politics – for this is no political matter – to do his best to help the Irish race to develop in future upon Irish lines, even at the risk of encouraging national aspirations, because upon Irish lines alone can the Irish race once more become what it was of yore – one of the most original, artistic, literary, and charming peoples of Europe.

From the speech by Douglas Hyde 'The Necessity for De-Anglicising Ireland', 25 November 1892

Question

This above extract is, in one sense, an outline of Hyde's rationale for the Gaelic League. In what sense could it be described as 'separatist' in its argument?

How successful was the League?

The main drive of the League was to promote the use of Irish in education. In that it was to prove successful. The League's newspaper *An Claidheamh Soluis* (*The Sword of Light*), which was set up in 1899, acted as a powerful advocate of the use of Irish in schools. In 1900–01 the League circulate over 100,000 copies of pamphlets arguing its causes. **The Boer War**, which ended in 1902, provided a stimulus to the League's popularity as a bastion of anti-imperialism. By 1906 the League had 75,000 members in 985 branches and had become a formidable pressure group. Yet it had not yet evolved into a revolutionary or a sectarian organisation; it was not until 1915 that the constitution of the Gaelic League was altered to state explicitly an adherence to a 'free Gaelic-speaking Ireland'. But

Definition

The Boer War

The Boer War was a colonial war fought between Britain and the Boer provinces of the Orange Free State and Transvaal Republic. The Boers were the descendents of Dutch settlers and they resented the spread of British rule.

there were many within the League who supported a separatist stance; from 1903 the future leader of *An Claidheamh* was Patrick Pearse. There was also tension between the League and the Irish Party. By 1908 Irish had become a part of the curriculum in National Schools but in 1909 there was considerable debate as to whether it should be a compulsory entry requirement for the new National University. One of the critics of such an idea was the deputy leader of the Irish Party, John Dillon. The following extract is from the *Weekly Freeman's Journal*, which was a strongly nationalist newspaper.

Source D

After all, it is our university . . . and is it not wise, does it not tend to discredit our country, that now and for the first time a British government has met us fairly and given us an institution which we can control ourselves that we should select that opportunity to fall upon each other with fury for a detail?

It has been said and repeated that this is a fight between the friends and foes of the Gaelic revival. . . . To my knowledge many of those most strongly opposed to making Irish compulsory for matriculation in the new university are just as keen friends of the language and of the Gaelic movement as the most violent of the advocates of compulsory Irish. The question truly stated is not an issue between friends and foes of the Gaelic revival. It is a question of educational method.

John Dillon speaking to the National Convention, reported in the
Weekly Freeman's Journal, 20 February 1909

Question

Reading through Source D, what were Dillon's objections to Irish being made a compulsory part of matriculation into the National University?

Biography

Arthur Griffith (1871–1922)

Arthur Griffith was born in Dublin in 1871. In adult life he became a printer and in 1893 helped set up the Celtic Literary Society before working for a few years in South Africa. In 1899 he founded the *United Irishman* and in the following year he established the cultural body Cumann na nGaedheal, The main drift of his political philosophy was that Ireland should be self sufficient politically and economically. In 1905 he set up Sinn Féin and in the following years he worked closely with other separatist movements. In 1913 he joined the Irish Volunteers but was not an advocate of the use of force. Griffith argued against Irish people participating in the Great War and in December 1914 the newspaper *Sinn Féin* was banned.

Although he did not take part in the Easter Rising of 1916 he was imprisoned. He was later released to become President of the first Irish Parliament, the Dáil, in 1919. Griffith headed the Irish delegation at the Treaty of London negotiations (see pages 154–9) in 1921 but died in 1922.

What was Sinn Féin?

[handwritten: caused the creation of — created]

The cultural revival spawned political movements, which also focused on national identity, unity and ultimately independence. An important figure in this process was Arthur Griffith, editor of the newspaper *United Irishman* (set up in 1899) and founder, in 1900, of the cultural movement Cumann na nGaedheal. There was not much difference between Cumann na nGaedheal and other organisations such as the Gaelic League. Indeed, in 1903 Cumann na nGaedheal was represented at a National Convention, called to draw together the different parties of the separatist cause. What was distinct about Griffith's early political philosophy was his belief in abstentionism, that independence would come with a withdrawal from participation in and co-operation with British institutions including Parliament. The only institution that Griffith believed should tie Britain and Ireland together was the monarchy. Griffith received his inspiration from the relationship between Austria and Hungary.

[handwritten margin note: Cumann nGaedheal]

Source E

When you look around today and see Hungary freer and stronger and more prosperous than Austria, when you know that if Hungary declares itself a republic tomorrow – which she intends to do when the sad old man in Vienna dies [Griffith is referring to Emperor Joseph I] – Austria would not fight, because she could not – you may well rub your eyes, reflecting that Hungary never once sent a Parliamentary Party to Vienna to 'fight on the floor of the House' for home rule, never once admitted the right of Austria to rule over her, never once pretended to be 'loyal' to the power that had smitten her. . . .

From an article by Arthur Griffith published in the *United Irishman* 2 January 1904

SKILLS BUILDER

What comparisons between Ireland and Britain does Griffith invite the reader of this article to make?

Biography

Thomas Davis (1814 to 1845)

This is a reference to Young Irelander Thomas Davis who had a strong influence on Ireland's cultural landscape for the second half of the nineteenth century. Davis stressed the importance of the Irish language to the Irish national identity and the supreme importance of the national struggle.

[handwritten: was made insignificant]

In 1905 Griffith launched the Sinn Féin political party but it was to have limited impact on the Irish until the outbreak of the First World War. It is important to stress that separatist politics were not popular before 1914 and they had little impact. In 1908 a Sinn Féin candidate stood in a by-election in the North Leitrim constituency and won over 1,000 votes. In reality, Sinn Féin was marginalised by the continuing popularity of the Irish Party and the great debate surrounding Home Rule. Griffith personally opposed the use of violence in politics and, for that reason, left the IRB in 1910. His support for monarchy put him at odds with others in the separatist camp. Whereas Griffith believed in drawing into the cultural revival all sections of Irish society, he was criticised by those such as D.P. Morgan who, through the pages of the nationalist newspaper *The Leader* (set up in 1900), defined the Irish nation and 'Irishness' as being essentially Catholic.

Source F

It has been hinted to us that it is our opinion that no one but a Catholic can be an Irishman. We never said so, nor do we think so. . . . We are prepared to be perfectly frank with our sympathisers who think that we are 'too Catholic'. We have great admiration for Thomas Davis, but his 'Tolerance' scheme did not work . . . When we look out on Ireland we see that those who believe in Ireland are, as a matter of fact, Catholics. When we look back on history we find also, as a matter of fact, that those who stood during the last three hundred years for Ireland as an Irish entity were mainly Catholics, and that those who sought to corrupt them and trample on them were mainly non-Catholics. . . .

Such being the facts, the only thinkable solution of the Irish national problem is that one side gets on top and absorbs the other until we have one nation, or that each develops independently.

From D.P. Morgan *The Leader* published on 27 July 1901

Discussion point

Get into discussion groups. Given what you know about the course of Irish history up to 1901, what impact would Morgan's ideas have on the debate about Ireland's future?

Biography

James Connolly (1868–1916)

James Connolly was born in Edinburgh to Irish parents in June 1868. Raised in relative poverty he joined the British Army aged 14 but deserted in 1891. By this time he had become a committed socialist and in 1892 he became secretary of the Scottish Socialist Federation. In 1896 he travelled to Dublin and founded the Irish Socialist Republican Party, which aimed for political and economic freedom. In 1903 he emigrated to the USA but returned to Ireland in 1910, and in October 1911 he led the famous Belfast Textile Workers' strike. In 1913 he led the workers in the Dublin Lock-out and was instrumental in setting up the Citizen Army to defend workers against attacks. He opposed the war effort and set up an Anti-War Committee to oppose recruitment and conscription with the motto 'We serve neither King nor Kaiser, but Ireland' (see Source G). Connolly helped organise the Easter Rising and had an input in the drafting of the Proclamation of Independence. He was badly wounded in the fighting in the General Post Office during the Easter Rising. He was sentenced to death by the Military Tribunal for his role in the Rising and was executed by a firing squad in Kilmainham Gaol at dawn on 12 May 1916.

What was the significance of the 1913 lock-out in Dublin?

In the summer 1913, an industrial dispute broke out in Dublin; the course and resolution of which was to have an important impact on events which followed. The Employer's Federation led by wealthy businessman William Martin Murphy attempted to **lock-out** members of the Irish Transport and General Workers' Union. The lock-out was a bitter affair, with Irish political life divided. As hunger and even starvation hit the families of the locked-out workforce, so Larkin proposed sending worst affected children to England, a plan that backfired with the bitter condemnation of the Catholic Church:

- **Anti-strike** Against the strike were lined up the leadership of the Irish Party and groups such as the Ancient Order of Hibernians who were used by Murphy to physically attack the strikers. Many within the Catholic clergy condemned Larkin's and Connolly's tactics.

- **Pro-strike** A number of intellectuals lined up behind the strikers including W.B. Yeats, and leading members of the IRB including Patrick Pearse, Joseph Plunkett, Thomas MacDonagh and Eamon Ceannt.

Perhaps the most significant development of the dispute was the creation of a paramilitary force, the Irish Citizen Army. Created in 1913, it was to add another military force on to the streets of Dublin.

Definition

Lock-out

This is when employers lock their factories to prevent their workers from coming to work.

Source G

6.2 Headquarters of the ITGWU, October 1914.

SKILLS BUILDER

We have been given the date of this photograph but precious little else.

As an historian investigating the Ireland of late 1914, what conclusions could you draw from this photograph?

Given the source's weak attribution, how reliable is it as evidence?

Biography

Patrick Pearse (1879–1916)

Patrick Henry Pearse was born into a Catholic middle class family in 1879. He trained as a lawyer but did not practise the law. In 1895 he joined the Gaelic League and became editor of its paper, *An Claidheamh Soluis* ('*Sword of Light*'). Pearse believed in the need for the Irish people to return to a Gaelic way of life and he set up a school called St Enda's in September 1908 to promote these ideas. The curriculum of St Enda's was based around Irish culture and legends including that of the mythical Irish warrior Cú-Chulainn. Pearse became a member of the Irish Volunteers in 1913 and travelled to the United States in February 1914. It is in his meetings with revolutionary republicans such as John Devoy that Pearse became convinced of the need for a symbolic military Rising. Pearse returned to Ireland and played a full part in the preparations for the Easter Rising. On 23 April 1916, the Military Council of the IRB appointed Pearse Commandant-General of the Army of the Irish Republic and President of the Provisional Government, which was to be proclaimed the next day. Pearse was sentenced to death in the aftermath of the Rising. He was executed by firing squad in Kilmainham Gaol on 3 May 1916.

Why did the Irish Volunteers split in 1914?

On the outbreak of war, Redmond chose to pledge his loyalty and that of his party to the Crown in its hour of need. This decision was not so surprising; Home Rule had been granted and Redmond was keen to play his part as a senior statesman in what was an hour of unprecedented crisis. In pledging Ireland's loyalty, he acted in the same vein as the leaders of other British Dominions and his actions were designed with the hope that they would reassure unionists throughout Ireland. What became more controversial in Ireland was his pledging the loyalty of the Irish Volunteers, in a speech on 20 September 1914, to fight for the Crown outside Ireland.

Source H

'The interests of Ireland – of the whole of Ireland – are at stake in this war. This war is undertaken in the defence of the highest principles of religion and morality and right, and it would be a disgrace for ever to our country and a reproach to her manhood and a denial of the lessons of her history if young Ireland confined their efforts to remaining at home to defend the shores of Ireland from an unlikely invasion, and to shrinking from the duty of proving on the field of battle that gallantry and courage which has distinguished our race all through its history. I say to you, therefore, your duty is twofold. I am glad to see such magnificent material for soldiers around me, and I say to you: "Go on drilling and make yourself efficient for the Work, and then account yourselves as men, not only for Ireland itself, but wherever the fighting line extends, in defence of right, of freedom, and religion in this war"'.

John Redmond speaking to members of the Irish Volunteers at Woodenbridge, Co. Wicklow, 20 September 1914

Source I

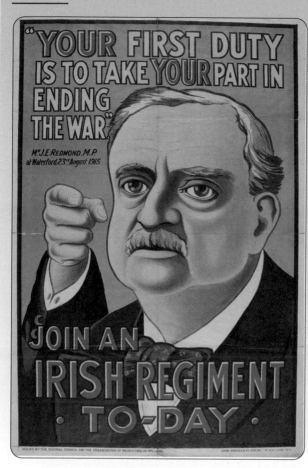

6.3 A recruitment poster showing John Redmond from August 1915.

Source J

At the next meeting of the Provisional Government we shall propose . . . To oppose any diminution of the measure of Irish self-government which now exists as a statute on paper, and which would not have reached that stage but for the Irish volunteers . . . To repudiate any undertaking by whomsoever given, to the legislative dismemberment [break up] of Ireland . . . To declare that Ireland cannot, with honour or safety, take part in foreign quarrels otherwise than through the free action of a National Government of her own; and to repudiate the claim of any man to offer up the blood and lives of the sons of Irishmen and Irishwomen to the service of the British Empire.

Manifesto of the Irish Volunteers, 24 September 1914

What was the impact of Redmond's speech?

The vast majority of the Irish Volunteers supported Redmond, between 150,000 and 170,000 forming themselves into the National Volunteers. A small minority of around 10,000 and essentially those influenced by the Irish Republican Brotherhood broke away keeping the name Irish Volunteers. Coming under the influence of radicals such as Eoin MacNeill in Dublin, the Irish Volunteers issued their manifesto soon after Redmond's speech at Woodenbridge.

What was Ireland's contribution?

However, around 80,000 Irishmen heeded Redmond's call and enlisted into the British Army in the first twelve months of the war. In addition to these figures should be added the 20,000 Irishmen already serving in the British Army when war broke out. Of the 80,000 new recruits, around 40,000 came from Ulster. The Irish soldiers were to serve throughout the war with great distinction. Redmond's hope was that the National Volunteers would be incorporated as a group into the British Army and turned into a distinct army corps. That did not happen, in part because of the suspicion of the Secretary of State for War, Lord Kitchener, who did not trust Irish

SKILLS BUILDER

In what ways and why does the opinion of Source J differ from that of Sources H and I?

Catholics. In contrast, the UVF who also volunteered to fight for the Crown, were incorporated as the 36th (Ulster Division). The Ulster Division became famous for the great bravery with which they fought and the huge losses they sustained at the Battle of the Somme in 1916. It should also be noted that large numbers of Irish women volunteered to support the war effort, including serving as VAD nurses.

As the war progressed, so the number of Irish men and women volunteering to serve the Crown reduced. One reason was the high death toll on all fronts that became apparent from early on in the war. On the first day of the offensive at Gallipoli, the Royal Dublin Fusiliers led the storming of the beaches at Cape Helles. Of the 25 officers and 987 other ranks to disembark for the shore, only one officer and 374 soldiers made it onto the beaches. As manpower dwindled, so the British government looked to introduce conscription across the United Kingdom in January 1916. A successful intervention from Redmond prevented the government insisting on conscription in Ireland, for such a move would have been unpopular and politically disastrous for the Irish Party who had placed such an emphasis on Irish people volunteering to serve. The tone of the campaign to recruit new soldiers in Ireland can be seen in this recruitment poster from 1916.

Source K

6.4 *The Call to Arms*, a poster encouraging volunteers to fight for the British Army, 1916.

John Redmond called a meeting of the Irish Party MPs to a conference to discuss how they might stimulate recruitment of Irish men and women to the war effort. The response from MP William Doris shows how many in the country responded to the call to arms.

Source L

As to the western part of the county, I fear we have very little chance of getting recruits, and the calling of public meetings would only show our weakness in this respect. On all questions (but this important question of the hour) the vast majority of people are with the party.

Most of our young fellows emigrate as they grow up and the small landowners will not listen to a suggestion that any of their few remaining sons should enlist. The Protestant farmers' sons in this district are even more hopeless slackers than our own people. Our shop assistants – mostly small farmers' sons – became such extreme nationalists all in a moment that they could not dream of 'fighting for England', and they are now regarded as Sinn Féiners.

From William Doris MP to John Redmond MP, 8 March 1916.
Doris is writing about the situation in County Mayo.

SKILLS BUILDER

Compare Sources J, K and L. What picture do they present of the problems faced by the government and the Irish Party in encouraging recruitment for the British Army in 1914 and 1915?

What was the significance of Patrick Pearse?

From 1914 the Irish administration in Dublin Castle turned a blind eye to the drilling and marching of the Irish Volunteers led by Eoin MacNeill. The priority of the moment was the need to continue to enlist soldiers for the war effort. Revolutionary republicans centred in the IRB recognised that this was a chance too good to be missed on the basis of the old Fenian mantra 'Ireland's opportunity is England's adversity'. In 1915 members of the IRB took control of the Gaelic League with leading member of the IRB Military Council, Thomas Clarke, taking control. The IRB also used the Irish Volunteers as a cover to prepare for a Rising in 1916. One of the leaders of the Volunteers, Patrick Pearse, joined the IRB in 1915 and was co-opted onto the IRB's Supreme Council and the Secret Military Council.

from MacNeill in 1914 – drilling and marching at administration at dublin castle turned a blind eye

Pearse has been identified as the leader of the Easter Rising, as much for the fact that, as a writer, he was committed to the idea of heroic self sacrifice. In his writings for newspapers such as *Irish Freedom* and in his own poems and prose, Pearse provided revolutionary nationalism with the appropriate language of rebellion and sacrifice. He also provided them with numerous sound bites which were to resonate in years to come if not at the time. At the funeral of Fenian leader O'Donovan Rossa in 1915, Pearse's graveside speech ended with the much quoted words, 'Ireland unfree shall never be at peace'. The last pamphlet written by Pearse in March 1916 (see Source M) gives a flavour of his political thinking.

patrick pearse wrote this

Source M

There is no other sort of nationalism than this, the nationalism which believes in and seeks to enthrone the sovereign people . . . the gentry have uniformly been corrupted by England, and the merchants and middle-class capitalists have, when not corrupted, been uniformly intimidated, whereas the common people have for the most part remained unbought and unterrified. It is, in fact, true that the repositories of the Irish tradition, as well the spiritual tradition of nationality as the kindred tradition of stubborn physical resistance to England, have been the great, splendid, faithful, common people; that dumb multitudinous throng which sorrowed during the penal night, which bled in '98, which starved in the Famine; and which is here still; what is left of it: unbought and unterrified. Let no man be mistaken as to who will be lord in Ireland when Ireland is free. The people will be lord and master. The people who wept in **Gethsemane**, who trod the sorrowful way, who died naked on a cross, who went down into hell, will rise again glorious and immortal, will sit on the right hand of God, and will come in the end to give judgment, a judge just and terrible.

From Patrick Pearse *The People Who Wept in Gethsemane*, March 1916.

Definition

Gethsemane
This is the garden where, according to the Bible, Jesus and his disciples withdrew to pray after the last supper and the night before Jesus's crucifixion. In the garden of Gethsemane, Jesus was full of anguish knowing the events of the day ahead.

How did the influence of Pearse and Connolly combine?

James Connolly's influence, especially on Pearse, was to outlast the lockout and strike in Dublin in 1913. A meeting was held in September 1914 between Connolly, Pearse and other Fenian leaders. The importance was his belief that an Irish nation state needed to be established before there could be any form of social or economic justice. To that end, his views were to match those of the nationalist Fenians. From 1914 onwards, a number of members of the Citizen Army were to join the IRB and socialist and nationalist were to come together to fight the nationalist cause. In January 1916, the Military Council of the IRB won Connolly's support for the military Rising later in the year. In February 1916, Connolly explained his political philosophy;

Source N

For the sake of a few paltry shillings per week thousands of Irish workers have sold their country in the hour of their country's greatest need and greatest hope. For what is the reason for the presence of the English army in this country? The sole reason for the presence of such soldiers in Dublin, in Ireland, is that they may be used to cut the throats of Irish men and women should we dare demand for Ireland what the British Government is pretending to fight for in Belgium. Like a poisonous ulcer this tie of self-interest has spread over Ireland corrupting and destroying all classes, from the Lord Mayor in his Mansion House to the poor boy and girl in the slum. Corrupting all hearts, destroying all friendships, poisoning all minds.

And yet the great heart of the nation remains true. Some day most of those deluded and misled brothers and sisters of ours will learn the truth, some day we will welcome them back to our arms purified and repentant of their errors . . . But deep in the heart of Ireland has sunk the sense of the degradation wrought upon its people – our lost brothers and sisters – so deep and humiliating that no agency less potent than the red tide of war on Irish soil will ever be able to enable the Irish race to recover its self-respect, or establish its national dignity.

Without the slightest trace of irreverence but in all due humility and awe we recognise that of us as of mankind before **Calvary** [see page 119] it may truly be said: 'Without the Shedding of Blood there is no Redemption.'

From James Connolly *Notes From The Front: The Ties That Bind*, 5 February 1916

SKILLS BUILDER

Compare Sources O and N.

How much of Pearse's influence can you read in this extract by Connolly?

How much of Connolly's influence can you read in this extract by Pearse?

What happened during the Easter Rising?

In early 1916, the IRB Military Council was divided as to the best course of action for a Rising:

- On the one hand were the more idealistic such a Pearse and Connolly who believed that a gesture of defiance against the British needed to be made, whatever the consequences.

- The more pragmatic including Eoin MacNeill believed that a Rising should only be attempted when conditions were right.

In the end, the more idealistic had the upper hand on the IRB's Military Council and for much of early 1916, their main task was not so much preparing for the Rising but keeping their plans secret from their more pragmatic colleagues. One potential source of aid was Germany. Since 1914, Irish Volunteer Sir Roger Casement had been in Germany trying to raise support for an Irish Brigade from Irish prisoners of war. Casement's hope was that the Brigade would win Germany's goodwill and support for the cause of Irish independence. The number of volunteers for the 'Irish Brigade' was very small and Casement's attempts at persuading Germany to arm the insurgents failed. Days before the Easter Rising, the Royal Navy intercepted the German ship *Aud* and its cargo of 20,000 rifles and 10 machine guns off the coast of County Kerry. Casement was arrested after landing in County Kerry, was tried and was hanged as a traitor in London in August 1916.

The Rising took place on Easter Monday, 1916. Lack of organisation, poor planning and lack of support from Eoin MacNeill meant that risings outside Dublin failed to materialise, apart from in north County Dublin and a few other isolated incidents. The aim of the 1,300 Irish Volunteers and 300 members of the Citizen Army in Dublin were to win support for their cause as events unfolded. The rebels seized the General Post Office and a few other strategically important buildings nearby, including Boland's Mill, the Four Courts, the South Dublin Union and at St Stephen's Green. The military leadership for the Rising was provided by James Connolly and Joseph Plunkett but the driving force for the proclamation of an Irish Republic and the main author of the statement of the declaration of the Republic was Pearse (although both Connolly and Plunkett contributed to its wording).

Definition

Calvary

This was where Jesus Christ was crucified.

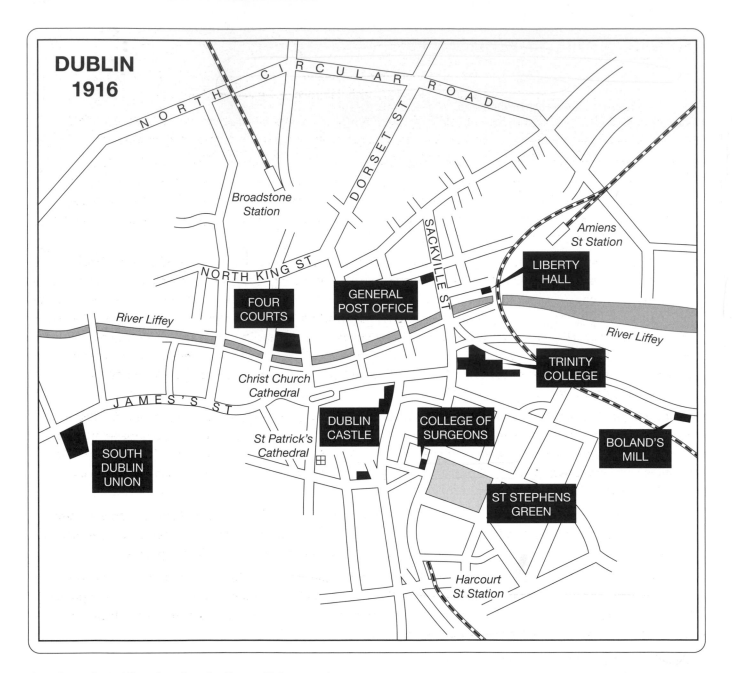

6.5 Places in Dublin related to the Easter Rising, 1916.

SKILLS BUILDER

Study the Proclamation closely.

What are the points made by the authors of the Proclamation?

What indications are there in the Proclamation that shows that this is from the separatist strand of republicanism?

Source O

Poblacht na h-Éireann
The Provisional Government of the Irish Republic to the People of Ireland

IRISHMEN AND IRISHWOMEN: In the name of God and of the dead generations from which she receives her old tradition of nationhood, Ireland, through us, summons her children to her flag and strikes for her freedom.

Having organised and trained her manhood through her secret revolutionary organisation, the Irish Republican Brotherhood, and through her open military organisations, the Irish Volunteers and the Irish Citizen Army, having patiently perfected her discipline, having resolutely waited for the right moment to reveal itself, she now seizes that moment, and, supported by her exiled children in America and by gallant allies in Europe, but relying in the first on her own strength, she strikes in full confidence of victory.

We declare the right of the people of Ireland to the ownership of Ireland, and to the unfettered control of Irish destinies, to be sovereign and indefeasible. The long usurpation of that right by a foreign people and government has not extinguished the right, nor can it ever be extinguished except by the destruction of the Irish people. In every generation the Irish people have asserted their right to national freedom and sovereignty; six times during the last three hundred years they have asserted it to arms. Standing on that fundamental right and again asserting it in arms in the face of the world, we hereby proclaim the Irish Republic as a Sovereign Independent State, and we pledge our lives and the lives of our comrades-in-arms to the cause of its freedom, of its welfare, and of its exaltation among the nations.

The Irish Republic is entitled to, and hereby claims, the allegiance of every Irishman and Irishwoman. The Republic guarantees religious and civil liberty, equal rights and equal opportunities to all its citizens, and declares its resolve to pursue the happiness and prosperity of the whole nation and all of its parts, cherishing all of the children of the nation equally and oblivious of the differences carefully fostered by an alien government, which have divided a minority from the majority in the past.

Until our arms have brought the opportune moment for the establishment of a permanent National, representative of the whole people of Ireland and elected by the suffrages of all her men and women, the Provisional Government, hereby constituted, will administer the civil and military affairs of the Republic in trust for the people.

We place the cause of the Irish Republic under the protection of the Most High God. Whose blessing we invoke upon our arms, and we pray that no one who serves that cause will dishonour it by cowardice. . . . In this supreme hour the Irish nation must, by its valour and discipline and by the readiness of its children to sacrifice themselves for the common good, prove itself worthy of the destiny to which it is called.

Signed on Behalf of the Provisional Government.
Thomas J. Clarke,
Sean Mac Diarmada, Thomas MacDonagh,
P.H. Pearse, Eamonn Ceannt,
James Connolly, Joseph Plunkett

Declaration of the Irish Republic, 24 April 1916

Once the British authorities had recovered from the initial surprise of Easter Monday they moved in to crush the Rising. By 29 April it was clear that the Rising was doomed to military defeat. The sacrifice sought by Pearse and his colleagues had been considerable with 450 killed, of whom 250 were civilians caught up in the fighting or killed while looting shops in and around Sackville Street. Although Pearse surrendered to the British military authorities in the afternoon of 29 April, in one sense the IRB had achieved one of its aims in that the Rising started a process of radicalisation that spiralled out of control of the British and played into the hands of the more militant revolutionary nationalists.

Source P

6.6 British soldiers inside the ruins of the General Post Office after the Easter Rising, 1916.

SKILLS BUILDER

What are the strengths and weaknesses of this postcard as evidence of the events of the Easter Rising?

What was the public reaction to the Rising?

There was initial confusion in Ireland as to who was responsible for the Rising. Martial Law was imposed immediately and a Military Governor, General Maxwell, appointed. Maxwell's initial reaction was *'to arrest all Sinn Féiners'*, which was based on the widely held assumption that Sinn Féin was responsible. Some members of Sinn Féin did indeed take part as individuals but neither the leadership or the party were officially involved. Because the authorities were not too sure who was behind the Rising, around 3,500 people suspected of being revolutionary nationalists were arrested. Many of these were detained under the terms of the **Defence of the Realm Act** passed in 1914. Of those arrested, around 1,800 were imprisoned without trial in Britain. This large number of arrests had an impact on public opinion, turning many people from being passive in their attitude towards the Rising to being actively sympathetic. Likewise, the well publicised actions of a few British troops on the streets of Dublin in the wake of the Rising had an impact, notably the shooting by a British Officer of a well-known Home Ruler Francis Skeffington who was trying to prevent looting.

The initial response in Dublin to the Rising was mixed. Many Dubliners had relatives fighting in the First World War and their response was scorn for the rebels. The majority of the casualties in the fighting were Irish and, for many, the Rising was an attack on the Irish people. Frank O'Connor was a 13-year-old child living in Cork at the time; he eventually became a famous writer of short stories. His recollections, written in his memoirs around forty years later, were of horror at events as they unfolded.

Other Dubliners took advantage of the chaos surrounding the Rising to engage in looting. Ernie O'Malley was an 18-year-old medical student who became caught up in the violence of the Easter Rising, joining in sniping at British troops. He eventually became a leading member of the IRA, writing his memoirs in the 1930s.

Source Q

The daily papers showed Dublin as they showed Belgian cities destroyed by the Germans, as smoking ruins inhabited by men with rifles and machine guns. At first my only reaction was horror that Irishmen could commit such a crime against England. I was sure that phase had ended with the Boer War in which father had fought, because one of his favourite songs said so – 'You used to call us traitors because of agitators but you can't call us traitors now'.

From Frank O'Connor *An Only Child* published in 1958

Source R

Little girls hugged teddy bears and dolls as if they could hardly believe their good fortune. Kiddies carried golf bags and acted as caddies to young gentlemen in bright football jerseys and tall hats, who hit golf balls with their clubs, or indeed anything that came in their way. This was a holiday. Some of the women with wispy, greasy hair and blousy figures walked around in an evening dress.

From Ernie O' Malley *On Another Man's Wound* published in 1936

The belief that the Rising was a treasonous betrayal became a view widely shared in Britain. Soon after the Rising, the following picture appeared in the *Illustrated London News*. It was drawn by R. Caton Woodville who was a famous and talented war artist and illustrator. The soldiers depicted in the picture are Irishmen fighting on the Western Front.

Source S

THE REAL IRELAND: THE HEROISM OF THE IRISH SOLDIERS FIGHTING FOR THE EMPIRE.

DRAWN BY R. CATON WOODVILLE FROM A WAR OFFICE OFFICIAL FILM.

"SAYING WHAT THEY THINK OF TREASON AT HOME": IRISH TROOPS ON THE WESTERN FRONT LEAVING THEIR TRENCHES AND CHARGING TO TAKE ENEMY TRENCHES.

6.7 *Saying What They Think of Treason at Home* published in *Illustrated London News*, Easter 1916.

SKILLS BUILDER

Using Sources Q, R and S and your own knowledge, what were the immediate reactions in Ireland and Britain to the Easter Rising in 1916?

Case study: What was the public reaction to the executions?

The leaders of the Easter Rising were imprisoned in Kilmainham Gaol. They were tried by Military Tribunal on the instructions of General Maxwell. The critical turning point of the Rising came with the execution of fifteen of its leaders in Kilmainham Gaol between 3 May and 12 May. Those executed included Pearse, Connolly and Tom Clarke. Below is a selection of evidence explaining the public's reaction to the executions. Study the evidence carefully and then answer the questions.

Source T

The fifteen grisly executions in early May created as many martyrs. The case in law, given the German connection, was conclusive for the death penalty; but in the circumstances of Ireland during 1916, the decision against **commutation** was inflammatory.

Rural Ireland, whose attitude towards separatist nationalism in 1915 had been found by Volunteer organizers a mixture of 'incredulity, suspicion and dour hostility', soon rediscovered traditional modes of resistance to established authority. Even more striking was the shift in 'respectable' opinion. The appalled reaction to the rising amongst the urban middle classes immediately afterwards . . . was rapidly moderated by the action of local garrisons; a survey of County Meath newspapers shows that by early 1917 Cumann na mBan and other extreme nationalist organisations were being given a new kind of respectful coverage.

From R.F. Foster *Modern Ireland 1600–1972* published in 1988

Definition

Commutation

This is the process of reducing a sentence to a less severe one.

Source U

6.8 *Erin's [Ireland's] Tragic Easter* by Francis Rigney, 1916.

Source V

. . . I asked the Prime Minister, first of all, whether he would give a pledge that the executions should stop. That he declined to give. Secondly, I asked him whether he could tell whether any executions had taken place in Ireland since Monday morning; the last we had official notification of before I left there. The reply of the Prime Minister was 'No, Sir, so far as I know, not'. On Monday twelve executions have been made public. Since then, in spite of the statement of the Prime Minister, I have received word that a man named Kent has been executed in Fermoy . . . The fact is one which will create a very grave shock in Ireland, because it looks like a roving commission to carry these horrible executions all over the country . . .

. . . It is the first rebellion that ever took place in Ireland where you had a majority on your side. It is the fruit of our life work. We have risked our lives a hundred times to bring about this result. We are held up to odium as traitors by those men who made this rebellion, and our lives have been in danger a hundred times during the last thirty years because we have endeavoured to reconcile the two things, and now you are washing out our whole life work in a sea of blood.

. . . The great bulk of the population were not favourable to the insurrection, and the insurgents themselves, who had confidently calculated on a rising of the people in their support, were absolutely disappointed, They got no popular support whatever. What is happening is that thousands of people in Dublin, who ten days ago were bitterly opposed to the whole Sinn Féin movement and to the rebellion, are now becoming infuriated against the government on account of these executions, and, as I am informed by letters received this morning, that feeling is spreading throughout the country in the most dangerous degree.

Speech of Nationalist John Dillon MP to the House of Commons,
16 May 1916

Source W

The executions, which followed the defeat of the Volunteers horrified the nation . . . The first open manifestation of the deep public feeling aroused by the executions was at the Month's Mind for the dead leaders. A Month's Mind is the Mass celebrated for the soul of a relative or friend a month after his death. It was the first opportunity that sympathisers of the rebels had to come out in the open. I went with my father to the first of the Month's Minds, which was for the brothers Pearse, at Rathfarnham. We arrived well in time for Mass but could not get into the church and the forecourt was packed right out to the road. I was surprised to see so many well-dressed and obviously well-to-do people present . . . I went to other Month's Minds with my father – to Merchant's Quay, John's Lane and other city churches. For us young people these Masses were occasions for quite spontaneous demonstrations, shouting insults at the Dublin Metropolitan Police who were always around but, having learned their lesson during the 1913 strike, were anxious to avoid trouble. . . .

By C.S. Andrews who eventually became a member of the Dublin IRA.
His memoirs, *Dublin Made Me,* were published in 1979.

Source X

I have met them at close of day
Coming with vivid faces
From counter or desk among grey
Eighteenth-century houses.
I have passed with a nod of the head
Or polite meaningless words,
And thought before I had done
Of a mocking tale or a gibe
To please a companion
Around the fire at the club,
Being certain that they and I
But lived where motley is worn:
All changed, changed utterly:
A terrible beauty is born.

Too long a sacrifice
Can make a stone of the heart.
O when may it suffice?
That is Heaven's part, our part
To murmur name upon name,
As a mother names her child

When sleep at last has come
On limbs that had run wild.
What is it but nightfall?
No, no, not night but death;
Was it needless death after all?

For England may keep faith
For all that is done and said.
We know their dream; enough
To know they dreamed and are dead;
And what if excess of love
Bewildered them till they died?
I write it in a verse –
MacDonagh and MacBride
And Connolly and Pearse
Now and in time to be,
Wherever green is worn,
Are changed, changed utterly:
A terrible beauty is born.

Easter 1916 written by William Butler
Yeats, 25 September 1916

SKILLS BUILDER

Preparatory thinking

- What are the points of agreement between Sources V and W and Sources U and X?

- How useful is Source X in telling the historian about attitudes towards the Easter Rising in Ireland in 1916?

Biography

William Butler Yeats (1865–1939)

Yeats was born into a Protestant family in 1865. The fact that his formative years were spent in the years when the Protestant Ascendancy was being directly challenged was to have a considerable impact on Yeats. Influenced by the work of Percy Bysshe Shelley and William Blake, he began writing poetry in earnest in the mid-1880s. He became involved in the cultural revival in the 1890s and in 1904 helped set up the Abbey Theatre in Dublin, which was to serve as a nerve centre for the revival. His poems, such as 'September 1913' and 'Easter 1916', reflect his understanding of the new nationalism that emerged in Ireland in this period. He served as a Senator in the Irish Free State and was awarded the Nobel Prize for Literature in 1923.

Unit summary

What have you learned in this unit?

From the late nineteenth century, a more militant nationalism re-emerged in Ireland. For most of the period from 1900 to 1916, it remained as a peripheral and idealistic strand of nationalism. There is no doubt that, in 1914, the majority of Catholic Ireland hoped for Home Rule as a solution to the Irish Question, rather than a more radical solution. However, the cultural revival was to change attitudes and the separatist strand of nationalism came to the fore in the aftermath of the Easter Rising of 1916.

On the other hand, thousands of nationalists continued to support the British war effort on the Home Front and in the trenches.

What skills have you used in this unit?

You will have worked with the sources and, through their evaluation, have developed an understanding that things are not always as they seem! Declarations can be produced for, among other things, propaganda purposes. On the other hand, you will have remembered that some people remained true to their principles, no matter how buffeted by events. You will have studied the reaction to the events of 1916 in some depth and will have worked with useful eye-witness accounts.

Exam style question

This is the sort of question you will find appearing on the examination paper as a (b) question. You are asked to use only two sources with your own knowledge. You may be asked to use two sources and you may be asked to use three – so be prepared for either and don't be surprised! Remember, though, that if you choose a (b) question that asks you to use two sources, don't assume that this is an easier question than one that asks you to use three. The two sources will be 'meatier' and more complex than the three.

Study Sources T and Q and use your own knowledge.

Do you agree with the view that the Easter Rising and its immediate aftermath provoked greater hostility towards the British?

Exam tips

- The **structure** of the question is different from the (b) questions you have worked on previously in the Exam Style question sections. This time the 'view' isn't contained in one of the sources but is given in the question.
- You will see that the two sources (T and Q) are much **denser** and **more complex** than sources you have dealt with previously. This means that they will need very careful reading.
- **Think carefully about** what each source says about the popular nature of the Easter Rising and jot this down. You will need to refer to these notes when you make your plan.

Now draw up your plan.

- **Analyse** Sources T and Q for points that support and points that challenge the view that the Rising and its immediate aftermath provoked greater hostility towards the British.
- **Cross-reference** between the sources for points of agreement and disagreement.
- Use your **wider knowledge** both to reinforce and to challenge the points you have derived from the sources.
- Combine the points into an **argument** for or against the view given in the question.
- **Evaluate** the conflicting arguments by considering the **quality of the evidence used.**
- Reach a balanced, **supported conclusion**

SKILLS BUILDER

1 Study Sources G, I, K and S. Using these pictorial sources, how far is it possible to draw a conclusion about the attitude of the Irish people towards participation in the First World War?

2 What were the causes of the Easter Rising? Work in pairs or small groups. Compare your views with those of other students. How have you used the evidence to back your views? Can you reach a class consensus about the reasons for the outbreak of the Rising?

3 Also working in pairs or small groups – how successful was the leadership of John Redmond?

RESEARCH TOPIC

The Somme

As indicated earlier in this unit, the 36th (Ulster) Division played an extraordinary part in the battle of the Somme which started in 1 July 1916. Your task is to research their contribution to the battle and its significance for Irish politics.

7 Breakdown in relations 1916–21

What is this unit about?

This unit deals with the emergence of Sinn Féin as the most important nationalist movement in the wake of the Easter Rising. It looks at the growing challenge to British rule, both electorally and in terms of violence. The last section of the unit focuses on the Anglo-Irish War which lasted from 1919 to 1921.

Key questions

- How did Irish nationalism change in the period 1916 to 1921?
- What was the impact of the Anglo-Irish War of 1919 to 1921?

Historical health warning!

There is again the need to issue a historical health warning so that you do not get confused. There is chronological overlap between this unit and the next. The next unit addresses the development of the nationalist cause over the same period and then into the war. They have been separated out for reasons of clarity, but you will need to cross-reference between the two units in order to gain the fullest understanding of the dynamics of the period.

Timeline

1916

May	Lloyd George attempts to broker a deal between the Irish Party and Ulster Unionists
August	Roger Casement is executed

1917

February	Count George Plunkett wins Roscommon by-election
March	Joseph McGuinness wins Longford South by-election
June	Release of prisoners involved in Easter Rising under a General Amnesty
July	Irish Convention meets; Éamon de Valera wins Clare East by-election
October	Sinn Féin ard fheis (convention) reorganises the party and Eamon de Valera becomes President of Sinn Féin

1918

March	John Redmond dies
April	Military Service Act makes possible conscription in Ireland
	Mansion House Conference of parties in Ireland opposed to conscription
May	Sinn Féin leadership arrested in the so-called 'German Plot'
December	Sinn Féin triumph in General Election

1919

January	Anglo-Irish War begins
	Dáil Éireann meets for the first time
July	Sinn Féin and the IRA banned

1920
January	Sinn Féin victorious in local elections
October	Cork Mayor, Terence MacSwiney dies on hunger strike
November	Eighteen auxiliary soldiers killed by IRA at Kilmichael
December	Centre of Cork burned by auxiliaries

1921
May	Burning of Customs House in Dublin
July	Truce between IRA and British forces

What was the reaction to the Easter Rising?

The reaction to the Easter Rising in Britain was one of great concern. The Chief Secretary for Ireland, Augustine Birrell, addressed the House of Commons in May 1916 stating that he had misjudged Sinn Féin even though the Rising had not been the work of Sinn Féin. Birrell had simply got it wrong. *Punch* published the following cartoon soon after. The cartoonist is unknown; the most famous *Punch* cartoonist of the period, Sir John Tenniel had died in 1914. The 'brother-saint' referred to in the cartoon is St Patrick, the patron saint of Ireland. Legend has it that St Patrick banished snakes from Ireland.

Source A

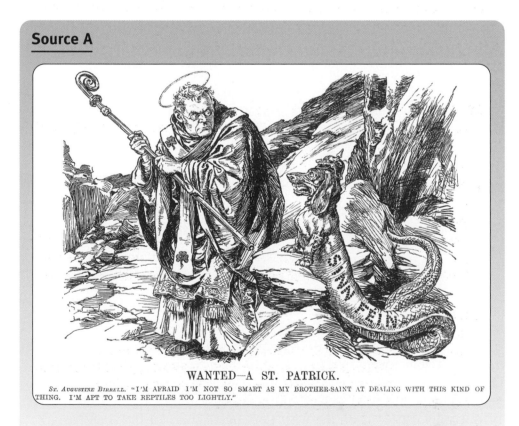

WANTED—A ST. PATRICK.

St. Augustine Birrell. "I'm afraid I'm not so smart as my brother-saint at dealing with this kind of thing. I'm apt to take reptiles too lightly."

7.1 *Wanted – A St Patrick*, published in *Punch* magazine, May 1916.

ST AUGUSTINE BIRRELL: 'I'm afraid I'm not so smart as my brother-saint at dealing with this kind of thing. I'm apt to take reptiles too lightly.'

SKILLS BUILDER

1 How is Sinn Féin depicted in this picture?

2 What are the similarities and differences in the how the Irish Question is portrayed between the *Punch* cartoon in Source A and the *Punch* cartoons of the nineteenth century?

From May 1915 to
December 1916, Herbert
Asquith led a coalition
government that included
members of the
Conservative Party (who
were unionists) and the
Labour Party.

On 12 May the Prime Minister Asquith travelled to Dublin to assess the situation for himself. One of the first consequences of his visit was that the executions of those involved in the Easter Rising were stopped and the sentences of the ninety-seven others due to be executed were commuted to terms of imprisonment. Asquith's response was to ask one of his Ministers David Lloyd George to try and resolve differences between unionists and the Irish Party over Home Rule. Between May and June 1916, negotiations took place. There was some shift in the Irish Party's position from the stance taken at the Buckingham Palace Conference (see pages 94–5). Redmond and the Belfast nationalist leader Joe Devlin persuaded northern nationalists that the only way for Home Rule to go ahead would be by accepting the temporary exclusion of six counties of Ulster. The decision was made at a conference of northern nationalists in Belfast in June 1916. The following source is written by Captain W.H. Owen, who was Lloyd George's 'eyes and ears' in Ireland; his job to investigate the main issues and to send Lloyd George regular reports. In June 1916 he travelled to Belfast to witness the debate about Home Rule and the proposed exclusion of six counties.

SKILLS BUILDER

1 What are the two
sides of the
argument
presented in this
source?

2 How reliable is this
source for an
historian finding
out about attitudes
of northern
nationalists
towards exclusion
of the six counties
from a Home Rule
solution?

Source B

On entering the hall I found the Very Rev. Canon Keown of Inniskilling speaking against the proposals . . . The speaker followed the common lines:

1 laying stress on the doubt as to the temporary nature of the scheme
2 suggesting that a separate executive was to be set up in Belfast, and
3 that an exhibition of courage and determination in opposing the present scheme, would result in other and more acceptable terms being offered by the Government.

Mr Joseph Devlin rose to speak . . . He firmly believed that if the proposals were adopted and an Irish Parliament set up in Dublin, the benefits attendant upon a scheme of that nature would soon become evident to the excluded counties and they would of their own accord very soon seek to be included under the jurisdiction of a Irish Parliament . . . It is not too much to say that Mr Devlin's words turned the tide in favour of the proposals.

From a report by W.H. Owen to Lloyd George, June 1916

Even though the Irish Party were prepared to compromise, the unionists in Asquith's Cabinet were not. In July 1916 the government announced that Lloyd George's initiative was at an end. This was a crushing humiliation for Redmond who had tried so hard to find a political way ahead. In November 1916, Daniel O'Leary won the West Cork by-election for the Irish Party. However, the decline in the electoral fortunes of the Irish Party thereafter

Biography

Éamon de Valera (1882–1975)

Éamon de Valera was born in 1882 in the United States of America but was brought up in Ireland. After leaving college he became a mathematics professor. In 1908 he joined the Gaelic League and in 1913 he became a member of the Irish Volunteers. Committed to armed rebellion, de Valera was sworn into the Irish Republican Brotherhood (IRB) in 1915 and he was a commandant during the Easter Rising. Imprisoned after the Rising, he was spared execution because the army felt that it had executed enough of the Rising's leaders as well as the fact that he held an American passport. De Valera was imprisoned in England but released as part of a general amnesty in June 1917. After his release he was elected MP for East Clare, President of Sinn Féin and the Irish Volunteers. In May 1918, de Valera was arrested in the so-called 'German Plot' but he escaped from Lincoln Gaol in 1919, was elected as President of the first **Dáil Éireann** and then went to the United States for a year to raise money for the new Republic. De Valera did not participate in negotiations with the British government at the end of the Anglo-Irish War and he rejected the terms of the Anglo-Irish Treaty signed in December 1921. He led the anti-Treaty forces in the subsequent Irish Civil War. De Valera was to serve as both Taoiseach and President of Ireland before his death in 1975.

Definition

Dáil Éireann

This is the name for the Irish Parliament.

reflected the rapidly changing political attitudes which swept Ireland in the wake of the Easter Rising.

How popular was separatist nationalism in 1917?

A series of spectacular by-election victories in 1917 by nationalists who supported the idea of complete separation from Britain provided the impetus for further political change. These candidates stood on a platform of abstentionism, that they would not take up their seats in Westminster if elected:

- In February 1917, Count George Plunkett, an Independent with Sinn Féin support, won the by-election in North Roscommon. Plunkett's son, Joseph, had been one of those executed after the Rising in 1916.

- In May 1917, Joe MacGuinness, who had fought in the Easter Rising and was imprisoned in Lewis Gaol, won the by-election in Longford South. What was so significant about this victory was that MacGuinness was backed by William Walsh, Archbishop of Dublin.

- In July 1917, Éamon de Valera won the by-election at East Clare. The constituency seat had become vacant on the death of Willie Redmond, brother of John Redmond. Willie Redmond had died leading Irish troops at the Battle of Messines Ridge on the Western Front in Belgium.

However, despite their successes, there was no organised and structured political movement. The next source tells the historian much about the fluidity of the political situation at the time. The author, Mary MacSwiney, was a separatist republican from Cork.

Source C

You are a 'trump-card' at present, you know. There are all over the country many earnest and convincing and, in their way, sincere politicians who would like to play that 'trump-card' [use Plunkett's name] and win, but I assure you that the only friends it is safe to trust the organisation of an independent Ireland to must be sought – in Cork – in the ranks of the Volunteers and Cumann na mBan. . . . Unless your executive [of any future party or organisation] is composed mainly of them and controlled by them it cannot succeed. Any man who was prominent here either as an O'Brienite or a Redmondite will not command the confidence of the country.

From a letter by Mary MacSwiney to Count Plunkett, May 1917

What was the significance of the ard-fheis, October 1917?

Definition

Ard-fheis

An ard-fheis is a party conference.

Despite growing support for those such as Count Plunkett, there was, at the end of the summer 1917, still no political party or movement that represented all of the strands of separatist nationalism. In October 1917, Sinn Féin held its tenth **ard-fheis**. The conference marked a significant turning point in the history of the party and Irish politics. Up until 1916, Sinn Féin had been a political party based mainly on cultural nationalism. It had not been at the forefront of the Easter Rising, despite the widespread misunderstanding that it had been. As Irish Volunteers returned from internment in England in the summer of 1917 to public support and sympathy and as Sinn Féin backed candidates continued to perform so strongly in by-elections, so it was clear that some kind of realignment of the political perspective of the nationalist community was possible. This realignment would marry the two strands of separatist nationalism; the threat of violence with the ballot box. At the ard-fheis in October 1917, Éamon de Valera was elected as President of Sinn Féin and Arthur Griffith was chosen to be vice President.

From now on, Sinn Féin was to stand for the establishment of an independent Irish Republic. Once that had been achieved, the Irish people would be able to decide on their preferred form of government. There was discussion about the desirability of further uprisings but Griffith's preferred course of action was to convince the international community of the justness of nationalist calls for independence. His views were reported in the *Cork Examiner* in October 1917.

Source D

Ireland's claim to be at the Peace Conference was based on a doctrine of international law, the doctrine of suppressed sovereignty [the denial of right for people to rule their own country] . . . Their case was strong and must be heard. It could only be heard on two conditions. The first was that they destroy the representation that at present existed in the English Parliament. The very existence of that representation in the English Parliament denied Ireland's claim to sovereign independence. . . . In addition, they must have in Ireland before that Conference met, and the sooner they had it the better, a constitutional assembly chosen by the whole of Ireland which could speak in the name of the people of Ireland . . .

From the *Cork Examiner*, 26 October 1917

SKILLS BUILDER

How accurately do you think the *Cork Examiner* has represented the views of Sinn Féin?

Case study: What was the Irish reaction to the British government's attempt to impose conscription?

On 21 March 1918, the German armies launched their great Spring Offensive on the Western Front. The Allied armies were pushed back over forty miles with considerable losses. This turn of events was to further damage the position of the Irish Party as a number of regiments made up of National Volunteer soldiers such as the 6th Connaught Rangers were decimated in the fighting. Even more significant was the attempt made in April 1918 by the British Prime Minister David Lloyd George to extend conscription to Ireland with the introduction of a Military Service Bill. The Bill proposed giving the government the power to introduce conscription in Ireland without debate. His attempt to sweeten acceptance of conscription with a promise of immediate Home Rule seemed cynical. The wider context to Lloyd George's Bill explains why he was prepared to make such a proposal:

- Britain and her allies were on the brink of military defeat in the Great War.
- Other members of the Empire including Canada and Australia had introduced conscription.

For reaction to the Conscription Bill, study the following sources:

Source E

7.2 John Dillon on a platform at an anti-conscription rally in Ballaghaderreen, County Roscommon during the Conscription Crisis of 1918.

Source F

I have no part in politics and no liking for politics, but there are moments when one cannot keep out of them. I have met nobody in close contact with the people who believes that conscription can be imposed without the killing of men, and perhaps of women . . . it seems to me a strangely wanton thing that England, for the sake of fifty thousand Irish soldiers, is prepared to hollow another trench between the countries and fill it with blood. If that is done England will only suffer in reputation, but Ireland will suffer in her character, and all the work of my life-time and that of my fellow-workers, all our effort to clarify and sweeten the popular mind, will be destroyed and Ireland, for another hundred years, will live in the sterility of her bitterness.

From a letter by poet and writer W.B. Yeats to Lord Haldane, May 1918

Source G

Ireland appears at the present moment to be solidly united against conscription from north to south – I fancy that there is equal antipathy to it in Ulster, although a certain number of people engaged in shipbuilding may possibly speak in favour of it, knowing that they are safe [from being conscripted]. With the exception of one or two wounded men returned from the front, I have not heard one word in favour of it, but on the contrary, bitter hatred is shown by all classes of people other than the class which may be known as 'Society'.

From a military point of view, the game appears to be hardly worth the candle – it can only be justified by results. I am convinced that there would be the very greatest difficulty getting the conscripts, and when you have got them, I believe they will do more harm than good to the Army, and be of more trouble than they are worth. The general attitude appears to be one of passive resistance on the part of every single individual, and every obstacle will be put in the way that the ingenuity of Irish men and women can devise.

From a Report on the Present State of Ireland, Especially with Regard to Conscription, *written by the Duke of Atholl or Lloyd George and the War Office, 29 April 1918*

SKILLS BUILDER

Using Sources E, F and G, answer the following questions:

1 To what extent do Sources E and F support the impression given about the extent of support for conscription given in Source G?

2 Which of these three sources do you find most reliable in explaining the Conscription Crisis? Explain your answer fully with reference to all three sources.

What was the 'German Plot'?

The reaction of the British government to the anti-Conscription campaign was to arrest its leaders. On 17 May 1918, the viceroy in Dublin, Lord French, ordered the arrest of seventy-three Sinn Féin leaders including de Valera and Griffith on the grounds that they had were part of a German plot to undermine Britain. The evidence in favour of such a plot was that it also served to stoke up further resentment, driving those who had been previously moderate in their viewpoint into the hands of Sinn Féin. The following extract is written by a member of the Irish Party who was a Protestant and Member of Parliament for Donegal. The extract was published in the *Contemporary Review*, which was a long-established and highly respected journal:

Source H

The tension is extraordinary, and the wildest stories find belief. Thus the visit of a single RAMC officer to a disused workhouse which it was thought might serve for a convalescent home at once produced a rumour that 500 soldiers had arrived in the district to commence a drive for conscripts; and quick on its heels came the statement that these were Gurkhas, specially trained to hunt men through the mountains and kill them with knives. To Englishmen it may well seem incredible that fellow-subjects of theirs should credit their rulers with intentions such as are here implied. Nevertheless, it is not only peasants who believe that the aim of an influential section here and in Ireland is not so much to gain recruits for the Army as to find a pretext for a pogrom in which the troublesome aspirations of Ireland after self-government may be once and for all quenched in blood, and the work half-done by Cromwell completed. To this pass has a country come which in August 1914, was the 'one bright spot on the horizon'.

By Hugh Law from the *Contemporary Review* published in June 1918

What were the results of the *'Coupon Election'*, 1918?

The General Election of December 1918 marked the formal end of the electoral dominance of the Irish Party. The Representation of the People Act 1918 had given the vote to all men over 21 and women over 30 with certain qualifications, thereby increasing the size of the electorate to 2 million (in 1910 it had been 700,000). But the Conscription Crisis and the supposed 'German Plot' gave Sinn Féin a huge electoral boost. Sinn Féin stood on a platform that appealed to a sufficiently broad section of the population. Some of the issues were mainstream radical nationalist issues such as some land issues.

Definition

'Coupon Election'

During the First World War, the Liberal Party split between the followers of David Lloyd George, who led the coalition government from December 1916 to the end of the war and the official leader of the Liberal Party, Herbert Asquith. In the run up to the General Election of 14 December 1918, the 159 Liberal candidates supporting Lloyd George were sent a joint letter of backing from Lloyd George and Andrew Bonar Law, leader of the Conservative Party. It was Asquith who nicknamed the letter a 'coupon' (there was still rationing at this time). In time the election was also given the same nickname.

Source I

IS IRELAND A PART OF ENGLAND?

On April 12th, CAPTAIN D.D. SHEEHAN said in the English House of Commons:

"I know all the English arguments. They only take account of English politics. It is quite natural they should only take account of England's politics, but they are all founded upon the English delusion that Ireland is part of England."

If Ireland is not a part of England, why should Irish Members attend the English Parliament, especially when they are outnumbered there 6 to 1?

VOTE FOR SINN FEIN
AND SHOW THE WORLD THAT IRELAND IS NOT A PART OF ENGLAND

7.3 A Sinn Féin Campaign poster, 1918.

Definition

Peace Conference

The Peace Conference referred to in Sinn Féin's manifesto was the Versailles Conference, which met at the end of the First World War. One of the most important leaders to attend the Versailles Conference was American President Woodrow Wilson. His proposals, known as the Fourteen Points, suggested that all peoples should be able to determine, through democracy, their nation state.

SKILLS BUILDER

Sources I and J are both from election materials. Does this mean that they are less reliable as evidence of Sinn Féin's policies?

Source J

Sinn Féin aims at securing the establishment of [the Irish] Republic.

1 By withdrawing the Irish representation from the British parliament and by denying the right and opposing the will of the British government or any other foreign government to legislate for Ireland.
2 By making use of any and every means available to render impotent the power of England to hold Ireland in subjection by a military force or otherwise.
3 By the establishment of a constituent assembly comprising persons chosen by Irish constituencies as the supreme national authority to speak and act in the name of the Irish people, and to develop Ireland's social, political and industrial life, for the welfare of the whole people of Ireland.
4 By appealing to the **Peace Conference** for the establishment of Ireland as an independent nation. At that conference the future of the nations of the world will be settled on the principle of government by consent of the governed.

Sinn Féin stands less for a political party than for the nation; it represents the old tradition of nationhood handed on from dead generations; it stands by the Proclamation of the Provisional Government of Easter, 1916, reasserting the inalienable right of the Irish people to achieve it, and guaranteeing within the independent nation equal rights and equal opportunities to all its citizens.

Sinn Féin's Manifesto to the Irish People written for the December 1918 election

Victory for Sinn Féin and the creation of Dáil Éireann

The General Election resulted in a huge victory for Sinn Féin. Out of the 105 seats, Sinn Féin won seventy-three with the Irish Party winning only six. Sinn Féin won just under 48 per cent of the national vote but there were huge regional variations. In the predominantly Catholic west of Ireland, Sinn Féin won twenty-five constituencies because their candidates were unopposed. The Irish Party's vote held up in some areas including in and around Dublin. But in reality, it had been overtaken by Sinn Féin, which was now the popular expression of Irish nationalism. The party of John Redmond was finished.

Sinn Féin claimed to be the inheritors of the tradition of Parnell; mixing the threat of violence with parliamentary politics. But the seventy-three Sinn Féin MPs (excluding those in British gaols) elected to Parliament in December 1918 took their seats on 21 January in Dáil Éireann in Dublin and declared the birth of the Irish Republic. De Valera was chosen to be President and Griffith as vice President. The declaration of a Republic surprised Griffith who had not envisaged an immediate and complete separation from Britain. However, the Dáil quickly set about creating Town and County Councils which, as they were dominated by Sinn Féin, looked to the Dáil rather than Westminster as the legitimate Irish Parliament. They also created so-called 'arbitration courts', to hear court cases.

Biography

Michael Collins (1890–1922)

Michael Collins was born in October 1890 in County Cork. In 1906 he went to live in London, subsequently joining Sinn Féin in 1908, the IRB in 1909 and the Irish Volunteers in 1914. Collins believed in violence as the best means of ending British rule in Ireland and he helped to organise the Easter Rising. Collins did not take part in the fighting but was imprisoned in England. On his release in December 1916, he returned to Ireland. Because of his financial skills, he was chosen to be Minister of Finance in the self-styled Irish Republic in April 1919. He also masterminded the IRA's campaign during the War of Independence; creating a 'Squad' of hitmen known as the 'Twelve Apostles'. After the war, Collins was one of the delegates who travelled to London to negotiate the Anglo-Irish Treaty signed in December 1921. The Treaty accepted the Partition of Ireland, for Collins it being the first step to a 32-county Ireland. After signing the Treaty, Collins wrote to a close friend: '. . . I tell you this – early this morning I signed my own death warrant'.--

Collins led the pro-treaty group of nationalists becoming Chairman of the Provisional Government and Minister for Finance in the Dáil government as well as Commander-in-Chief of the pro-treaty army. Civil War broke out between supporters and opponents of the Treaty and, on 22 August 1922, Collins was assassinated at Béal na mBláth near Macroom in County Cork.

The Anglo-Irish War 1919–21

Sinn Féin had not stood on a platform of violence in December 1918. However, in January 1919, armed conflict between Irish nationalists and British forces in Ireland, a conflict which was to be become known as the Anglo-Irish War, began.

The war can be divided into three main phases:

Phase 1: January 1919 to January 1920

The first phase of the war was fought as a terrorist war by members of what had been called the Irish Volunteers but was now called the Irish Republican Army. On 31 January 1919, the IRA declared that a state of war existed between Ireland and Britain. Therefore, they argued, their actions should not be treated as acts of terror but legitimate acts of war.

Source K

The principle means at the command of the Irish people is the Army of Ireland, and that Army will be true to its trust. If they are called on to shed their blood in defence of the new-born Republic, they will not shrink from the sacrifice. For the authority of the nation is behind them, embodied in a lawfully constituted authority whose moral sanction every theologian must recognise, an authority claiming the same right to inflict death on the enemies of the Irish State, as every free national government claims in such a case. Dáil Éireann, in its message to the Free Nations, further declares that the state of war can never be ended until the English military invader evacuates our country, a fact which has been recognised and acted on by the Volunteers almost from their inception.

We have thus a clear issue laid down, not by any body that could be termed 'militarists' or 'extremists', but by the accredited representatives of the Irish people met in solemn session, in a document drawn up with the utmost care and a full sense of responsibility, and unanimously adopted.

The 'state of war', which is thus declared to exist, renders the National Army the most important national service of the moment. It justifies Irish Volunteers in treating the armed forces of the enemy – whether soldiers or policemen – exactly as a National Army would treat the members of an invading army. It is necessary that this point should be clearly grasped by Volunteers.

Every volunteer is entitled, morally and legally, when in the execution of his military duties, to use all legitimate methods of warfare against the soldiers and policemen of the English usurper, and to slay them if it is necessary to do so in order to overcome their resistance. He is not only entitled but bound to resist all attempts to disarm him.

From the IRA journal, *An t-Oglach*, 31 January 1919

Their chosen targets were members of the police force, the Royal Irish Constabulary (RIC). To the IRA, the RIC were the representatives of British authority in the country. The reality was more complex; 70 per cent of the RIC were Catholics and often the RIC constable was the mainstay of the local community. The campaign of terror in 1919, did not win universal support from the Catholic Church or from many within Sinn Féin who hoped that the Versailles Treaty would deliver self-determination for Ireland. Indeed, it was not until April 1921 that Sinn Féin took full responsibility for the actions of the IRA. By the end of 1919, eighteen policemen had been killed.

There is often considerable difference between the realities of conflict and how it is portrayed subsequently. The Anglo-Irish War began with the murder of two Irish police officers at Soloheadbeg in January 1919. At the time, the murders caused considerable unease among politicians of all political persuasions, including some leaders of Sinn Féin. In later years, the actions of the assassins became to be commemorated.

Source L

SOLOHEADBEG MEMORIAL
Commemorating the Ambush at Soloheadbeg
21 January 1919

Unveiled by the President of Ireland
SEAN T. O CEALLAIGH
On Sunday 22 January 1950

There is a saying: 'Where Tipperary leads all Ireland follows'. This saying is well borne out by what followed the lead given the country at Soloheadbeg on Tuesday, 21 January, 1919, the day on which the first Dáil Éireann unanimously adopted the Declaration of Irish Independence. On that date an engagement took place between members of the Irish Volunteers and an armed enemy party, resulting in two RIC constables being shot dead and their equipment and arms, and the explosives they were escorting, captured. It is our proud claim for Soloheadbeg, that it was the first deliberate planned action by a select party of Irish Volunteers (shortly to be recognised as the Irish Republican Army) renewing the armed struggle, temporarily suspended, after Easter Week 1916. The men who took part in the Solohead ambush broke so far with tradition that they refused to fly the country after their coup. This course was urged upon them, but they determined to remain and carry on the fight against the enemy wherever and whenever they could, and with ever-increasing intensity. Their lead was an incentive to the rest of the country, and before long the British were finding that they had stirred up a hornet's nest.

From an Official Souvenir about the Soloheadbeg Memorial published in 1950

SKILLS BUILDER

What impression does this source give about the Soloheadbeg incident?

The violence against the RIC had its desired effect. The next source is by a member of the British Army who was in Ireland at the time.

SKILLS BUILDER

What, according to the author of Source M, was the impact of the IRA violence on members of the RIC?

Source M

The RIC were at this time distributed in small detachments throughout the country, quartered in 'barracks', which consisted, in the vast majority of cases, of small houses adjoining other buildings, quite indefensible and entirely at the mercy of disloyal inhabitants. The ranks of the force had already been depleted by murders, and many men, through intimidation of themselves or more often of their families, had been induced to resign. Although, in the main, a loyal body of men their moral [*sic*] had diminished, and only two courses were open to their detachments; to adopt a policy of laissez faire [leave things alone] and live, or actively to enforce law and order and be in hourly danger of murder.

Lieutenant-General Sir Hugh Jeudwine from 'Record of the Rebellion in Ireland in 1920–1921 and the Part Played by the Army in Dealing With It', written in 1922.

Phase 2 Early 1920 to the summer of that year

As the IRA's campaign against the RIC took its toll, IRA attacks on RIC barracks in the first half of 1920 resulted in the destruction of sixteen defended RIC barracks, damage to another twenty-nine, and the burning of 424 abandoned buildings to the ground. Many RIC officers left the force rather than face the increasing hatred of the local population. The response of the British government was to recruit ex-soldiers in Britain (known as **Black and Tans**) to serve in the RIC. They were effective in imposing martial law.

Definition

Black and Tans

The nickname Black and Tan came from the uniforms worn by the newly recruited soldiers. They wore dark green RIC caps and tunics with khaki trousers. This reminded people in Ireland of the uniform of a famous hunt from Limerick of the same name. By the end of the Anglo-Irish War, over 7,000 'Auxiliaries' or Black and Tans as they were nicknamed had served in Ireland. Those who joined the Black and Tans were mainly demobbed hardened non-commissioned soldiers.

Case study

Source N

7.4 'Black and Tans' searching a civilian.

Source O

They had a special technique. Fast lorries of them would come roaring into a village, the occupants would jump out, firing shots and ordering all the inhabitants out of doors. No exceptions were allowed. Men and women, old and young, the sick and decrepit were lined up against the walls with their hands up, questioned and searched. No raid was ever carried out by these ex-officers without their beating up with the butt ends of their revolvers, at least a half-dozen people. They were no respecters of persons and seemed to particularly dislike the Catholic priests.

From Tom Barry *Guerrilla Days in Ireland* published in 1962. Tom Barry was a prominent member of the IRA in Cork.

SKILLS BUILDER

1   What is the impression given of the Black and Tans in these Sources N and O?

2   What are the weaknesses of these sources taken as a set?

Source P

The truce had been a victory and a defeat for both sides. With it both sides acknowledged that they would prefer to fight no more. Inasmuch as the British Government were by far the stronger party and had always before been able to crush armed Irish rebellion, this represented a unique Irish victory. The government was treating its opponents as nominal equals. On the other hand they were not equals, and both sides knew it.

Far from having been able to drive the British out of Ireland, the IRA had been unable, as Mulcahy, the Chief of Staff, was soon to remind it, to drive them out of anything more than 'a fairly good-sized police barracks'. If it came again to a mere test of strength – and contingency plans for the introduction of 250,000 British troops and even a blockade of Ireland were being discussed – the IRA could never physically win. Moreover, in the sort of war the IRA had been fighting, a truce was much more harmful to their future capabilities than it was to that of regular professional forces.

From Robert Kee 'Ourselves Alone', published in the book *The Green Flag: The Turbulent History of the Irish Movement*, 1972

Phase 3 Summer 1920 to July 1921

The third phase of the Anglo-Irish War is associated with the actions of mobile IRA 'active service units', which were better known as 'Flying Columns'. It also was marked by growing concern in Britain about the violence in Ireland. In October 1920, Sinn Féin scored a great propaganda victory when the Lord Mayor of Cork, Terence MacSwiney died in Brixton Prison after seventy-four days of being on hunger strike. The IRA 'Flying Columns' took part in a number of high profile ambushes, including the killing of eighteen Auxiliary soldiers at Kilmichael in November 1920. The Minister of Finance in the Dáil, Michael Collins, was also Director of Intelligence for the IRA. On 21 November 1920, his gunmen scored a notable success in the assassination of twelve British Intelligence officers and two members of the Auxiliaries. The response from British forces was swift; later that day Auxiliary soldiers fired into a crowd at Croke Park killing twelve civilians. The day became known, not surprisingly, as 'Bloody Sunday'.

Source Q

7.5 *Sinn Féin Murder an Army Officer at Dublin.* Illustration by W.R.S. Stott published by the *Illustrated London News*, 11 December 1920.

SKILLS BUILDER

How does the artist of Source Q portray one of the assassinations on 'Bloody Sunday'?

The spiral of violent act and reprisal continued. In December 1920, Auxiliary soldiers burned the centre of Cork city in response to an IRA ambush. Concerns in Britain continued to be raised through organisations such as the Trades Unions and groups including the Anti Reprisals Committee and the Peace with Ireland Council. In May 1921, the IRA launched a large-scale attack on the Custom House in Dublin, which was home to Civil Service records. Such attacks came at a heavy price and, by mid-1921, the IRA was coming under increasing pressure, especially in Dublin and Cork. In June 1921, the Parliament of Northern Ireland was opened and Partition was a reality. The IRA was short of men and weapons but British public opinion had increasingly turned against Lloyd George's government because of the stories of atrocities committed in the name of the British government. Although weakened and increasingly on the back foot, the IRA had not been defeated. Indeed, de Valera had raised $5million in the United States of America in 1920 in support of the IRA's cause and the new and effective Thompson machine gun was being smuggled into the hands of the IRA from the United States in ever larger numbers.

On the basis of the fact that Partition was a reality (see pages 152–3), thereby satisfying the unionists in Westminster, some form of compromise with the nationalists in the south was possible. In May 1921, an election led to a virtual clean sweep for Sinn Féin outside the six counties that were now to become Northern Ireland. The King's speech opening the Northern Ireland parliament in June 1921 asking for 'conciliation' was the prelude to an agreement between Lloyd George and de Valera of a truce that came into force on 11 July 1921. Had the campaign of murder and terror and the counter-terror that followed it been worth it? This is a question that you might wish to discuss after reflecting on this unit and reading the next unit.

Conclusion

So this was it: after years of violence and bitter opposition, the more militant form of Irish nationalism had managed to switch the agenda from a devolution style Home Rule solution to **Dominion status**. The Anglo-Irish War had created popular myths mainly surrounding the IRA and the Black and Tans, which were to dominate for most of the rest of the century. The creation of the Dáil had been an important turning point and, by the summer of 1921, the loyalty of many courts and local councils in Ireland was to Dublin rather than London. It was not time for the negotiations to begin. However, whatever the success of the IRA in bringing the British government into negotiations, the issue of Northern Ireland was not on the table for discussion. Partition was a reality, as we will see in the next unit.

> **Definition**
>
> **Dominion status**
>
> This was the status held by other established members of the Empire, such as Canada and Australia. It meant that they were self governing but still had the British monarch as Head of State.

Unit summary

What have you learned in this unit?

You have learned how the First World War had an important effect on Irish politics, particularly through the Conscription Crisis. You have also learned how Sinn Féin emerged as the dominant Irish nationalist movement although its aims were still relatively ill-defined. At the heart of this unit is the development of a twin strategy of using the 'bullet and the ballot box'. You have learned about the Anglo-Irish War and how it ultimately led to negotiations. You have also read how Sinn Féin was increasingly successful in elections. The unit covers a period in Irish history that was to cause bitterness and stir emotion for decades to come.

What skills have you used in this unit?

You have evaluated source material in order to determine Irish reactions to the Conscription Crisis and the Black and Tans. You have tested the reliability of this evidence and, in some cases, you have highlighted its partisan nature.

Exam style questions

This is the sort of question you will find appearing on the examination paper as a (b) question.

Study Sources L and M and use your own knowledge.

Do you agree that it was the IRA's tactics that brought the British government to the negotiating table?

Exam tips

You have worked on (b) style questions at the end of other units.

You have experimented with different sorts of plans and considered different styles of question.

You should now have a good idea of the way in which you prefer to plan your answer. So go ahead and plan an answer to this question.

Now test yourself! Look at your plan and check what you have drawn up. Have you:

- **Analysed** Sources L and M for points that support and challenge the view that the IRA's tactics were successful in bringing the British to the negotiating table?
- Shown how you will **cross-reference** between the sources for points of agreement and disagreement?
- Shown where you will use your **wider knowledge** both to reinforce and challenge the points you have derived from the sources?
- Thought about how you will combine the points you have made into an **argument** for or against the view that the IRA's tactics brought the British to the negotiating table, and noted this on your plan?
- Shown how your **evaluation** of the points you have used in argument has considered the **quality of the evidence** used?
- Noted what your conclusion will be, and how you will ensure it is **balanced** and **supported**?

SKILLS BUILDER

1 One person's freedom fighter is another person's terrorist.
   This unit raises the issue of how acceptable is the use of violence
   in support of a political aim. Discuss with other people in your
   group, whether you believe that the violence of the IRA was
   justified or not.

2 On a related issue, the picture below was painted in 1921 by a Séan
   Keating. It is of an IRA Flying Column waiting to ambush a passing
   military vehicle. Keating painted the picture from sketches and
   photographs. Some of the North Cork Batallion of the IRA posed for
   Keating in Dublin after the truce of July 1921 was agreed. What
   impression does Keating give of the IRA and is he justified in
   doing so?

Source R

7.6 *Men of the South* (1921) by Séan Keating.

RESEARCH TOPIC

Michael Collins by Neil Jordan

In 1996, a film called (and about) *Michael Collins* was released. The film was made by Neil Jordan and was highly acclaimed. Neil Jordan claimed on a website promoting the film that:

> Collins wasn't a proponent of terrorism. He developed techniques of guerrilla warfare later copied by independence movements around the world. Collins would never be a proponent of contemporary terrorism as practiced today. He was a soldier and a statesman and, over time, a man of peace.

Try to see the film. After doing so, form yourselves into discussion groups and discuss the following points:

- From what you know, how accurate is the portrayal of the film?

- What are the problems for the historian using films such as *Michael Collins*?

8 Partition, the Free State and Civil War

What is this unit about?

This unit focuses on the events that led to the partition of Ireland by the Government of Ireland Act of 1920. It looks at the subsequent establishment of Northern Ireland. It also looks at the issues surrounding the Anglo-Irish Treaty of 1921 that attempted to provide a solution to the Irish Question. This unit explores the creation of the Free State, the different reactions to the Treaty in Ireland and the subsequent outbreak of civil war. It explains how the Free State won the civil war.

Key questions

- How was Ireland partitioned?
- Why did the Anglo-Irish Treaty of 1921 prove to be so controversial?

Timeline

1916

June	Ulster Unionist Council agrees to a six-county exclusion

1917

July	Irish Convention meets for the first time

1918

December	Unionists win twenty-six seats out of 105 seats in the General Election

1920

February	Government of Ireland Bill introduced into Parliament
March	Ulster Unionist Council accepts the Government of Ireland Bill
November	Enrolment begins of members of the Ulster Special Constabulary
December	Government of Ireland legislation put into practice in Northern Ireland

1921

February	James Craig becomes Ulster Unionist leader
May	General Election in Northern Ireland; Unionists win forty out of fifty-two seats
June	King George V opens Northern Ireland Parliament
July	Truce signed in Anglo-Irish War
October	Negotiations begin between Sinn Féin and the British government
December	Anglo-Irish Treaty signed

1922

January	Treaty accepted by the Dáil Éireann
March	Craig–Collins pact signed to reduce sectarian violence in Northern Ireland
June	General Election in Irish Free State; voters support Treaty
	Irish Civil War begins between pro- and anti-Treaty forces

	August	Michael Collins assassinated
	December	Irish Free State established
1923		
	May	End of the Civil War

Source A

THE KINDEST CUT OF ALL.

WELSH WIZARD. "I NOW PROCEED TO CUT THIS MAP INTO TWO PARTS AND PLACE THEM IN THE HAT. AFTER A SUITABLE INTERVAL THEY WILL BE FOUND TO HAVE COME TOGETHER OF THEIR OWN ACCORD—(ASIDE)—AT LEAST LET'S HOPE SO; I'VE NEVER DONE THIS TRICK BEFORE."

8.1 *The Kindest Cut of All*, a cartoon from *Punch* magazine, 10 March 1920. The cartoon was drawn by the cartoonist Bernard Partridge.

SKILLS BUILDER

What conclusions can you draw from this cartoon about attitudes in Britain towards the partition of Ireland?

What was the Irish Convention?

Those who had wished to find a constitutional settlement in Ireland continued to talk through the last months of the war. From July 1917 to April 1918, an Irish Convention met to try and find a way ahead that was acceptable to both nationalists led by John Redmond, the southern unionists led by Viscount Middleton and the northern unionists whose delegation was fronted by H.T. Barrie. There was a breakthrough at the Conference, the southern unionists agreeing to the idea of self-government for Ireland. This was the first time that they had accepted any form of Home Rule. However, by the time the Convention broke up, Redmond was dead and the German Offensive of March 1918 had opened up the issue of conscription. At no point during the Convention were the Ulster Unionists willing to consider any form of self-government for Ireland. But the fact that the southern unionists were prepared to accept some form of self-government increased the division between Ulster and southern unionists. The government now moved to consider the shape of Partition.

What was the Government of Ireland Act, 1920?

In October 1919, the Prime Minister David Lloyd George set up a Cabinet Committee led by **Walter Long** to consider the Irish Question. By December the Committee had made a number of decisions which Lloyd George explained to Parliament in a speech in December 1919. There are two very important issues covered and you will need to read the speech through very carefully.

Biography

Walter Long

Walter Long served as Chief Secretary for Ireland in 1905 and was a strong unionist. He also served as First Lord of the Admiralty, which was the job he held when asked by Lloyd George to chair the Cabinet Committee.

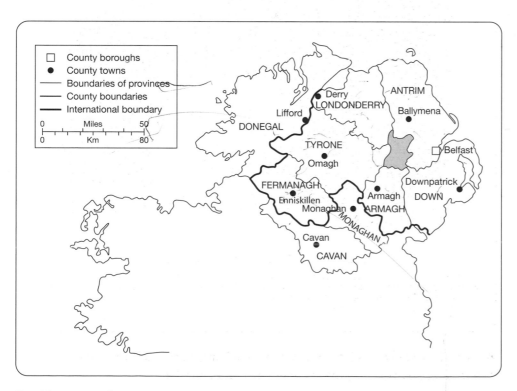

8.2 Ulster counties.

Source B

We propose that self-government should be conferred upon the whole of Ireland, and our plan is based on the recognition of those three fundamental facts:

- The first involves the recognition that Ireland must remain an integral part of the United Kingdom.
- The second involves the conferring of self-government upon Ireland in all of its domestic concerns.
- The third involves the setting up of two parliaments, and not one, in Ireland. One will be the Parliament of Southern Ireland; the other will be the Parliament of Northern Ireland.

There are four alternative proposals which have been discussed with regards to boundaries:

- The first is that the whole of Ulster should form one unit . . . The objection to that is that it would leave large areas where there is a predominantly Catholic . . . population.
- The second suggestion is county option. The objection to this is that it would leave solid communities of Protestants . . . under a government to which they are rootedly hostile.
- The next suggestion is that the North-Eastern counties should form a unit. There is the same objection to that, because there are solid Catholic communities in at least two of these counties.
- The fourth session is that we should ascertain what is the Northern-Eastern section, and constitute it into a separate area, taking the six counties as a basis, eliminating, where practical, the Catholic communities and including the Protestant communities from the neighbouring Catholic counties.

From a speech by David Lloyd George to the House Commons, *Hansard*, 22 December 1919

SKILLS BUILDER

1 What are the two main issues identified by Lloyd George and the options within those issues?

2 Some of these proposals are different from the proposals for Home Rule in 1914 (see Units 5 and 6, pages 83–129). Can you identify the differences?

The Government of Ireland Act, 1920

In February 1920, the government published the Government of Ireland Bill. Its main features were as follows:

- The creation of a six-county Northern Ireland that would also have its own executive and Parliament.
- A twenty-six-county Southern Ireland, which also was to have its own executive and Parliament.

While many Ulster Unionists were content to accept the proposals others were not. Protestants living in Donegal and Monaghan were unhappy at being left out of the newly created Northern Ireland. Other unionists had mixed feelings but in the end accepted that Partition as proposed protected their interests. Captain Charles Craig was the Unionist MP for County Down. In the following speech in Parliament he explains how, in the end, the Ulster Unionists saw positives in the proposals.

Source C

With the prospect of this bill passing into law, we Ulstermen find ourselves face to face with the most extraordinary paradox. While on the one hand our hatred and detestation of home rule and all connected with it is as great as ever was . . . yet on the other hand we do see in this bill the realisation of the objects which we aimed at when we raised our [Ulster] Volunteer Force in 1913 and 1914 . . . Because it gives Ulster a parliament of its own, and sets up a state of affairs which will prevent . . . for all time Ulster being forced into a parliament in Dublin without its own consent; because it does those two things I say that the bill practically gives us everything we fought for. . . .

From a speech by Captain Charles Craig to the House of Commons,
Hansard, 29 March 1920

SKILLS BUILDER

Summarise Captain Craig's analysis of the Government of Ireland Bill.

In December 1920, the Bill became law and elections were planned for the late spring of 1921. The Act provided for two Parliaments linked by a 'Council of Ireland'. Although the British government was keen to stress that Partition was temporary, the reality of the situation was different. An administration for Ulster was set up under the direction of Under-secretary for Ulster affairs, Sir Ernest Clark. In the elections to the Northern Ireland Parliament in May 1921, forty seats went to the Unionists, six to Sinn Féin and six to the Nationalists. The new Prime Minister was James Craig. His priorities were to consolidate the new state and defeat IRA violence. The means by which this was achieved were by creating the **Ulster Special Constabulary** and using the Royal Irish Constabulary to crush any potential military challenge.

What was the background to the Anglo-Irish Treaty?

In the previous unit you learned how a truce was called between the IRA and the British government. It was the opening of the Northern Ireland Parliament and the reality of Partition that created the context for the British government's more conciliatory attitude towards Sinn Féin. David Lloyd George was a highly skilled politician and an experienced negotiator. He understood that the creation of Northern Ireland undermined Sinn Féin's claim that they spoke for the whole of Ireland. The king's speech at the official opening of the Northern Ireland Parliament in June 1921, which called for conciliation, provided an opportunity to make a move to break the deadlock and cycle of violence. On 24 June, Lloyd George wrote to de Valera:

Definition

Ulster Special Constabulary

The USC was created in October 1920. There were three types of Special Constables: the most infamous were the part-timers known as the B Specials. The USC often used violence and intimidation against the nationalist community and were highly effective.

SKILLS BUILDER

1 What is the tone of Lloyd George's letter?

2 What does he suggest to de Valera?

Source D

Sir,

The British Government are deeply anxious that, so far as they can assure it, the King's appeal for reconciliation in Ireland shall not have been made in vain . . . They felt it incumbent upon them to make a final appeal, in the spirit of the King's words, for a conference between themselves and the representatives of Southern and Northern Ireland, I write, therefore, to convey the following invitation to you as the chosen leader of the great majority in Southern Ireland, and to Sir James Craig, the Premier of Northern Ireland:

(1) That you should attend a conference here in London, in company with Sir James Craig, to explore to the utmost the possibility of a settlement.
(2) That you should bring with you for the purpose any colleagues whom you may select. The Government will, of course, give a safe conduct to all who may be chosen to participate in the conference.

We make this invitation with a fervent desire to end the ruinous conflict which has for centuries divided Ireland and embittered the relations of the peoples of these two islands, who ought to live in neighbourly harmony with each other, and whose co-operation would mean so much not only to the Empire but to humanity.

We wish that no endeavour should be lacking on our part to realise the King's prayer, and we ask you to meet us, as we will meet you, in the spirit of conciliation for which His Majesty appealed.

I am, Sir, Your obedient servant,
D. Lloyd George

A letter from David Lloyd George to Éamon de Valera, 24 June 1921

The truce of 11 July was followed by a period of uneasy military standoff between the two sides. However, the truce held sufficiently for the two sides to begin to explore the possibility of a conference to resolve differences. On 12 July, a Sinn Féin delegation, consisting of de Valera, Arthur Griffith, Austin Stack and Erskine Childers, left for London. Their arrival in the British capital was to be followed by a series of one-to-one talks between de Valera and Lloyd George. The differences between the two sides were considerable:

- Lloyd George was only prepared to talk on the basis of Ireland holding Dominion status and with no promises of an end to Partition.
- De Valera claimed to full sovereign independence for an Irish Republic.

The initial talks in London failed and were followed by a series of letters written across the summer of 1921. The differences between the sides and problems faced Lloyd George are summed up in the following cartoons. The first cartoon is from *Punch* magazine and is drawn by an anonymous artist. It depicts Lloyd George considering the Irish Question. The reference to the Highlands is due to the fact that he stayed for much of the summer in Gairloch in the Scottish Highlands. The second cartoon is drawn by British artist David Low drawn in 1921. Low was to become the most famous political cartoonist of the twentieth century.

Source E

THE UNITED KINGDOM DRAMA IN 3 ACTS

THE PROBLEM PLAY.

OUR EVER-JEUNE PREMIER (*conning his part*): "NOW HERE AM I, A WELSHMAN, LOOK YOU: AND I HAF TO COME ON IN A HIGHLAND 'SET,' AND PLAY A SCENE IN ENGLISH—ALL ABOUT IRELAND—WITH A SPANISH AMERICAN—AND LEAD UP TO A HAPPY ENDING. WELL, WELL, I HOPE IT WILL BE ALL RIGHT ON THE NIGHT!"

8.3 'The Problem Play' published in *Punch* magazine, summer 1921.

Source F

HOITY TOITY! WE'LL NAME HER "SOVREIGN."
TUT TUT TUT! WE'LL NAME HER "DOMINION."
IRISH FREEDOM
DE VALERA
LOW

8.4 *What's in a Name Yap* by David Low, 1921.

SKILLS BUILDER

Explain the meaning of the cartoons in Sources E and F. How do they contrast? What are their similarities and differences?

Source G

We therefore send herewith a fresh invitation to a conference in London on 11 October, where we can meet your delegates and spokesmen of the people whom you represent, with a view to ascertaining how the association of Ireland with the community of nations known as the British Empire may best be reconciled with Irish national aspirations.

From a letter by David Lloyd George to Éamon de Valera, 29 September 1921

SKILLS BUILDER

De Valera accepted Lloyd George's invitation to a conference in London. However, on what terms was he accepting the invitation?

After an exchange of twelve letters between Lloyd George and de Valera, the latter signalled that Sinn Féin were prepared to enter talks, despite the fact that Lloyd George had made it very clear that he was not prepared to entertain the idea of an Irish Republic. Read the following Lloyd George's comments in his letter to de Valera.

Who were Sinn Féin's negotiators?

Despite being the leader of Sinn Féin, de Valera chose not to attend the London Conference. The reasons for his actions are many, some of which are explained in Source H. What is not explained is the fact that, by the autumn of 1921, de Valera's rivalry with Michael Collins over who was to be the leading figure in Sinn Féin had grown. Collins was included in the negotiating team to travel to London alongside Arthur Griffith (who was to be chairman of the delegation) and Robert Barton (Minister for Economic Affairs), two other members of the Dáil, George Gavan Duffy and Eamon Duggan, and secretarial assistance from Finian Lynch, Diarmuid O'Hegarty, John Chartres and Erskine Childers. The fact that Collins was to be in London and de Valera in Dublin gave the latter the advantage in that he could manipulate public opinion at home. The problem with this arrangement was that the delegates in London were supposed to pass all main decisions through the Cabinet in Dublin. Given the difficulties of communication between Dublin and London, this was easier said than done. At this time, the only reliable form of communication was by telegraph. This meant that, for the negotiators to have any meaningful discussion with de Valera or the Cabinet, they had to travel back to Dublin for face-to-face talks. In this extract of a letter to a sympathetic Irish-American, de Valera explains what he wanted from a settlement and the reasons why he stayed at home.

Source H

On my return from London, when it became necessary to send a written reply to the British proposals, I proposed another way out – external association of Ireland with the group of free nations in the British Empire. In entering such an association Ireland would be doing nothing incompatible with her declared independence. This proposal in its main outline was accepted by the [Dáil] Cabinet and the whole Ministry (about 15 members were present when I made it) and I set out with the fixed determination of making peace on that basis. Lest I might in any way compromise the position of the Republic, and in order that I might be in a position to meet any tricks of Lloyd George, I remained at home myself, but the plenipotentiaries had agreed with my view, had had their instructions and even a preliminary draft treaty to guide them.

From a letter by Éamon de Valera to Joseph MacGarrity, 21 December 1921

SKILLS BUILDER

1 What does de Valera claim were his proposals for a settlement?

2 What reasons does de Valera give for not going to London?

3 Source H is written after the peace treaty was signed by the British and Irish delegates. The terms of the treaty were not to de Valera's liking. What do you think is the purpose of de Valera's letter and how valuable is it to an historian investigating the events surrounding the Anglo-Irish treaty?

What were the issues facing the British delegation?

The British delegation was led by Lloyd George who was ably supported by his private secretary, Tom Jones. The British negotiating team was made up of political heavyweights including Austen Chamberlain, Winston Churchill and Lord Birkenhead. Such an experienced team placed considerable pressure on the Irish delegation to accept compromise on the two main issues of sovereignty and allegiance to the British Crown. In Dublin, de Valera continued to stress the importance of what he called 'external association'; that Ireland could remain within the British Commonwealth but with republican status. The reality was that such a proposal was unacceptable to the British and they were not prepared to compromise on the issue. Slowly but surely, Lloyd George and the British negotiating team wore the Irish team down. Collins and Griffith accepted the phrase 'free partnership with the other States associated within the British Commonwealth', in the belief that this would allow an Irish Free State to be associated with but remain outside the Commonwealth. The reality was that the British intended that the Irish Free State stayed within the Commonwealth.

The Irish delegation also looked for a resolution of the Ulster issue. The republicans hoped that Lloyd George would put pressure on the Ulster leader James Craig to agree to an all-Ireland parliament. The original intention of the Irish delegation was that they would withdraw from the talks if the issue of Ulster was not resolved in their favour. On 22 November, an 'Irish memorandum' outlined again the demands of the Irish delegation including 'external association'. However, serious divisions had emerged within the Irish delegation: Erskine Childers criticised the failure of the document to mention an independent republic. The British response was that they would not consider any proposal that did not include a symbolic role for the Crown in Ireland. The British submitted their proposals, which were discussed by the Cabinet in Dublin on 3 December. Collins and Griffith were instructed by the Cabinet to:

- stand by the idea of 'external association';

- reject the idea of an Oath of Allegiance to the British Crown;

- not to sign any agreement without reference to the Dáil.

The delegation returned to London under considerable pressure. Despite receiving orders from the Cabinet in Dublin, the reality for the delegation was that failure to come to an agreement might well lead to the resumption of the war. On 5 December, Collins and Lloyd George traded concessions, Lloyd George agreed to a Boundary Commission to reconsider Northern Ireland's borders. In return Collins hinted that the Irish delegation would agree to association with the Empire as proposed by the British. Talks continued with Lloyd George reminding them that Arthur Griffith had agreed to such a compromise in November. On this basis he pushed for an agreement, without further consideration of the Ulster issue or consultation with the Dáil. Failure to sign would result in war with the Irish delegation being blamed. Michael Collins was well placed to judge that the IRA would find it difficult to fight a renewed war, given shortages of ammunition and supplies and the possible size of any British force. After a short period of discussion, the Irish delegation agreed to sign the Treaty. The following two pieces of evidence are from the moment of final agreement:

Source I

I saw Arthur Griffith at midnight for an hour alone. He was labouring under a deep sense of the crisis and spoke throughout with the greatest earnestness and unusual emotion. One was bound to feel that to break with him would be infinitely tragic. Briefly his case was:

1 That he and Collins had been completely won over to belief in your desire for peace and recognised that you had gone far in your efforts to secure it. This belief was not shared by their Dublin colleagues and they had failed to bring them all the way, but were convinced they could be brought further. In Dublin there is still much distrust and fear that if the 'Treaty' is signed they will be 'sold'.

2 They are told that they have surrendered too much ('the King' and 'association') and got nothing to offer the Dáil in return. Cannot you – and this was the burden of his appeal – get from Craig a conditional recognition, however shadowy, of Irish national unity in return for the acceptance of the Empire by Sinn Féin? Will he [Craig] not write you a personal letter, as AG did, saying Ulster will recognise Unity if the south accepts the Commonwealth? Then the south will give all the safeguards you want for the north and will not ask for the boundary commission – a most difficult thing to give up. . . .

From a letter from Tom Jones to Lloyd George, 5 December 1921.
Tom Jones was Lloyd George's Private Secretary.

SKILLS BUILDER

1 What were the issues identified by Jones and Collins?

2 Reading Source J, why was Collins so desperate?

Source J

When you have sweated, toiled, had mad dreams, hopeless nightmares, you find yourself in London's streets, cold and dank in the night air. Think – what have I got for Ireland? Something which she has wanted these past seven hundred years. Will anyone be satisfied at the bargain? Will anyone? I tell you this; early this morning I signed my death warrant. I thought at the time how odd, how ridiculous – a bullet may just as well have done the job five years ago.

Michael Collins writing to his friend John O'Kane, 6 December 1921

How was the Treaty received?

The Treaty set up the Irish Free State. It gave the Irish Free State control over its domestic affairs and full Dominion status. In reality, this gave the Free State legislative independence; it could make its own laws. The Treaty set up a Boundary Commission to look into the border of Northern Ireland. However, it also included an Oath of Allegiance to the British Crown and a Governor General. The Irish Cabinet accepted the Treaty by four votes to three and it was then debated in the Dáil. There was mixed reaction to the Treaty in the Dáil with feelings running high on both sides. These are two extracts from speeches made in the Dáil debate.

Source K

. . . the provisions of this Treaty mean this: that in the north of Ireland certain people differing from us somewhat in tradition, and differing in religion, are going to be driven, in order to maintain their separate identity, to demarcate themselves from us. I heard something about the control they are going to exercise over the education of the republican minority in the north of Ireland? They will be driven to make English, as it is, the sole vehicle of common speech and communication in their territory, while we will be striving to make Gaelic the sole vehicle of common speech in our territory. And yet you tell me that, considering these factors, this is not a partition provision.

From a speech by Sean MacEntee on 22 December 1921. MacEntee was from Belfast.

Source L

Now Mr Griffith has referred to the difference between this Treaty of his and the alternative that we have as being only a quibble; and yet the English government is going to make war, as they say they will, for a quibble. The difference is, to me, the difference that there is between a draught of water and a draught of poison. If I were to accept this Treaty and if I did not do my best to have it defeated I would, in my view, be committing national suicide; I would be breaking the national tradition that has been handed down to us through the centuries. We would be doing for the first time a thing that no generation thought of doing before – wilfully, voluntarily admitting ourselves to be British subjects, and taking the oath of allegiance voluntarily to an English king.

From a speech by Cathal Brugha to the Dáil, 7 January 1922. Brugha was Minister of Defence and an opponent of Michael Collins, of whom he was jealous.

Why was the Irish Civil War fought?

Despite the objections of those such as Brugha and MacEntee, the Dáil voted to accept the Treaty on 7 January 1922 by a margin of sixty-four votes to fifty-seven. This vote reflected the majority opinion in the country.

Those who objected to the Treaty were headed by de Valera. In the light of the pro-Treaty vote he forced a vote of confidence in his presidency which he lost by two votes. A Provisional Government of the Free State was set up with Arthur Griffith as its leader. In the weeks and months that

SKILLS BUILDER

What are the objections to the Treaty expressed in Sources K and L?

Definition

The Four Courts

The Four Courts were highly significant as the centre of Ireland's legal system. It was where Dublin's main courts were situated and where the records were kept.

followed the Dáil's votes, both sides, pro- and anti-Treaty, sought ways of reconciling their differences. The pro-Treaty Michael Collins was put in charge of the committee set up to draft a constitution for the Free State. He attempted to draw both sides together by writing the Crown out of the new constitution. However, the British were not prepared to accept what was a radical revision of the Treaty and the initiative failed. In May 1922, de Valera and Collins agreed to an electoral pact for the up and coming General Election, the idea being that Sinn Féin would continue to hold the monopoly of political power. By the time of the election in June 1922, the pact had started to unravel and the electorate were clearly heavily in favour of the Treaty, with around 78 per cent of votes going to pro-Treaty candidates.

Those who opposed the Treaty showed that they were prepared to take direct action to bring the government of the Free State down. In April 1922, a number of IRA members, now known as Irregulars, seized the Four Courts in Dublin. Led by IRA member Rory O'Connor, their actions mirrored those of Patrick Pearse and the rebels of 1916. The Provisional Government of the Free State did not respond immediately, partly because of concerns about events in the north. In Northern Ireland, the tension between Ulster Unionists and nationalists had spilled over into violence. Collins twice met the Northern Ireland leader James Craig to try and find ways of ending the communal violence. However, the Craig–Collins Pact of March 1922 failed to have much impact on the situation. Ironically, one of the reasons why communal violence continued was an IRA campaign of murder in Ulster, which took place with the knowledge of Collins. As ever, Collins was playing a double game; on the one hand seemingly wishing to find a way of reducing violence but on the other hand promoting violence.

On 22 June 1922, the retired Field Marshall and outspoken Ulster Unionist, Sir Henry Wilson, was murdered in London by two IRA gunmen. The British put great pressure on the Provisional Government to deal with the republican military threat. Rather than risk the possibility of British military action in Ireland, the forces of the Provisional Government attacked republican forces holding the **Four Courts**. The Government's army, directed by Minister of Defence Richard Mulcahy, was better equipped and had the support of the majority of the population and the Catholic Church. They drove the Irregular forces westwards in the summer of 1922 and the war then took the form of the type of guerrilla conflict that characterised the earlier Anglo-Irish conflict. One of the victims of guerrilla attack was Michael Collins who was targeted and assassinated in an ambush in August 1922. Opposite is a photograph of his funeral procession.

Source N

8.5 Photograph of Michael Collins' funeral in Dublin, 28 August 1922.

How did the Provisional Government win?

The Provisional Government was also prepared to use brutal force to crush the Irregulars. On 24 November, the republican Minister of Propaganda, Erskine Childers, who had been captured earlier in the month was executed. After a pro-Treaty deputy at the Dáil, Seán Hales was assassinated in December, the Free State government executed four leading republicans Rory O'Connor, Liam Mellowes, Dick Barrett and Joe McKelvey. The Free State executed seventy-seven prisoners during the civil war, the impact being to wipe out the leadership of the Irregulars. In March 1923, a number of republican prisoners were killed in cold blood by their captors in County Kerry. The death of the Irregulars' leader Liam Lynch in April 1923 was the signal for the end of the war, the Irregular forces having been effectively defeated. The bitterness and hatred that the Civil War produced was to linger for decades. Up to 5,000 Irish people died in the conflict and thousands more had their lives ruined and property destroyed. The Irish Free State was born out of violence and bloodshed.

Unit summary

What have you learned in this unit?

You have learned that Ireland was partitioned by the Government of Ireland Act of 1920. The Anglo-Irish War was brought to a close and the search for a settlement involved lengthy discussion and correspondence between the two sides. You have learned that the Irish delegation to the peace talks was in a very difficult position. They ultimately gave way on the symbolic but important point of allegiance to the Crown. They were also unable to make headway over the issue of the future of Northern Ireland. The Anglo-Irish Treaty of 1921 represented in many ways a victory for Irish nationalism; the Dáil in Dublin was to have complete control over home affairs in the twenty-six counties of the South. While the Treaty was popular in the country as a whole, a minority perceived the adoption of the Treaty as an act of treachery. The Civil War that ensued was a tragedy, which rivalled many of the other tragedies in Irish history covered in this book.

What skills have you used in this unit?

You have used a range of source material to explore the issues surrounding Partition and the creation of the Irish Free State. The evaluation will have led you to understand that the creation of an independent Ireland was accompanied by bloodshed. You will have used sources dealing with the debate about the future constitutional structure of the South. A study of sources relating to the Anglo-Irish Treaty will have enabled you to use the skill of empathy to appreciate that the issues at the heart of the Treaty continued to be divisive.

SKILLS BUILDER

Change over a period of time

It is now time to reflect on the extent of change over the period covered by this book.

In your discussion group you should tackle the following issues.

For each of the following areas, explain what the situation was in 1867, what it was in 1922, and the extent of change over the period in question. If there has been significant change you try to explain why that change occurs:

- how Ireland is governed;

- the position of the British in Ireland;

- the nature of Irish nationalism;

- the nature of Ulster unionism.

Turning points

There were a number of turning points in the period covered by this book. An obvious one is 1916. What other turning points can you identify?

RESEARCH TOPIC

The Troubles

In the late 1960s a period of violence known as The Troubles started. They lasted for thirty years during which thousands of people in Britain and Ireland lost their lives. Your research task is to find out about The Troubles and how they were concluded.

Exam style question

This is the sort of question you will find appearing on the examination paper as an (a) question.

Study Sources K, L and M.

How far do Sources L and M reflect the views expressed in Source K that the Dáil should reject the Treaty?

You tackled (a) style questions earlier in this book. Now let's develop what you learned there about approaches to the (a) question.

Exam tips

- What is the question asking you to do? It is asking **how far** Sources L and M **support** Source K.
- Consider the sources carefully and make **inferences** and **deductions** from them rather than using them as sources of information. You might put these inferences in three columns.
- **Cross-reference** points of evidence from the three sources by drawing actual links between evidence in the three columns. This will enable you to make comparisons point by point and so use the sources as a **set**.
- **Evaluate** the evidence, assessing its quality and reliability in terms of how much weight it will bear and how secure are the conclusions that can be drawn from it.
- Reach a **judgement** about how far Sources L and M can be said to support Source K.

Exam zone

Relax and prepare

Hot tips: What other students have said

FROM GCSE TO AS LEVEL

I really enjoyed studying modern world History at GCSE level but I am glad that I had the chance to look at some nineteenth and twentieth century Irish and British history at AS level. It has been challenging but enjoyable to study a different period.

Many of the skills that I learned at GCSE level were built upon at AS level, especially in Unit 2 where the skills of source evaluation and analysis are very important.

The more practice source based questions I attempted, the more confident I became and quite quickly I picked up the necessary style and technique required for success.

AS level History seems like a big step up at first, with more demands made on independent reading and more complex source passages to cope with. However, by the end of the first term I felt as if my written work had improved considerably.

I found it really helpful to look at the mark schemes in the textbook. It was reassuring to see what the examiners were looking for and how I could gain top marks.

WHAT I WISH I HAD KNOWN AT THE START OF THE YEAR

I used the textbook a lot during the revision period to learn the key facts and practise key skills. I really wished that I had used it from the beginning of the course in order to consolidate my class notes.

I wished that I had taken more time reading and noting other material such as the photocopied handouts issued by my teacher. Reading around the subject and undertaking independent research would have made my understanding more complete and made the whole topic more interesting.

AS History is not just about learning the relevant material but also developing the skills to use it effectively. I wish that I had spent more time throughout the year practising source questions to improve my style and technique.

I wish I had paid more attention to the advice and comments made by my teacher on the written work I had done. This would have helped me to improve my scores throughout the year.

HOW TO REVISE

I started my revision by buying a new folder and some dividers. I put all my revision work into this folder and used the dividers to separate the different topics. I really took pride in my revision notes and made them as thorough and effective as I could manage.

Before I started the revision process, I found it helpful to plan out my history revision. I used the Edexcel specification given to me by my teacher as a guideline of which topics to revise and I ticked off each one as I covered it.

I found it useful to revise in short, sharp bursts. I would set myself a target of revising one particular topic in an hour and a half. I would spend one hour taking revision notes and then half an hour testing myself with a short practice question or a facts test.

I found it useful to always include some practice work in my revision. If I could get that work to my teacher to mark all the better, but just attempting questions to time helped me improve my technique.

Sometimes I found it helpful to revise with a friend. We might spend forty-five minutes revising by ourselves and then half an hour testing each other. Often we were able to sort out any problems between us and it was reassuring to see that someone else had the same worries and pressures at that time.

Refresh your memory: revision checklist

1 The Irish Question: key themes

- The Union and British rule in Ireland.
- Church and land.
- The impact of the Famine.
- Constitutional and revolutionary Irish nationalism.
- Unionism.

2 Land, 1867–85

- How was land distributed?
- What was the significance of agricultural depression in Ireland in the 1870s?
- What was the extent of rural violence?
- What was the impact of Michael Davitt and the Land League?
- Why did the government pass the Land Acts of 1870 and 1881?
- How effective was the policy of concession and coercion?

3 Violence and pacification, 1867–85

- What was Fenianism?
- What was the impact of the terrorist campaign in Britain in the 1880s?
- How did Gladstone attempt to 'pacify' Ireland 1868–74?
- Why did tensions in Ireland increase in the 1880s?

4 Home Rule and opposition, 1886–1905

- Why did Gladstone's convert to Home Rule?
- What was the impact of Gladstone's conversion on the Liberal Party?
- Why did the first and second Home Rule Bill fail?
- How widespread was unionism in the south of Ireland and Ulster?
- What was the impact on Irish nationalism of the fall of Parnell?

- What was the role played by Joseph Chamberlain and Lord Randolph Churchill?
- How successful was 'killing Home Rule with kindness'?

5 Third Home Rule Bill and Unionism, 1905–1914

- What role did John Redmond play?
- What was the Conservative Party reaction to the Third Home Rule Bill of 1912 (including the stance taken against it by Andrew Bonar Law)?
- What impact did the outbreak of war in August 1914 have on Home Rule?
- What was the role played by Edward Carson?
- How significant was the crisis of 1912 (including the creation of the Ulster Volunteer Force and Catholic Irish Volunteers in 1912)?
- What was the stance of the British Army in Ireland in 1914?

6 War and rebellion, 1914–16

- How significant were Arthur Griffith and Sinn Féin?
- What was the significance of the Gaelic League and Gaelic Athletic Association?
- What was the extent of Irish participation in the First World War?
- Why did the Easter Rising break out in 1916?
- What was the impact of the Easter Rising?

7 Breakdown in relations

- Why did attempts at a constitutional settlement in 1917 fail?
- How did attitudes towards the war change including the issue of conscription in Ireland in 1918?
- What was the significance of the outcome of the Coupon Election in 1918?
- How important was the creation of the Dáil Éireann in 1919?

- What were the roles played by Michael Collins and Éamon de Valera?
- What was the significance of the Anglo-Irish War of 1919–21(including the use of the Black and Tans and the use of martial law)?

8 Settlement and Civil War

- What were the main features of the Government of Ireland Act of 1920?
- What were the reasons for Partition and the creation of Northern Ireland?
- What was the impact of the Anglo-Irish Treaty of 1921?
- What were the causes and outcome of the Irish Civil War of 1922?

This revision checklist looks very knowledge based. The examination, however, will test your source-based skills as well. So remember that when dealing with sources you must be able to:

- Comprehend a source and break it down into key points.
- Interpret a source, drawing inferences and deductions from it rather than treating it as a source of information. This may involve considering the language and tone used as well.
- Cross-reference points of evidence between sources to reinforce and challenge.
- Evaluate the evidence by assessing its quality and its reliability in terms of how much weight it will bear and how secure are the conclusions that can be drawn from it. This may include considering the provenance of the source.
- Deal with the sources as a set to build a body of evidence.

Result

You have spent a lot of time working on plans and constructing answers to the (a) and (b) questions. So you now have a pretty good idea about how to plan an answer and write a response to the question of the examination paper. But what are the examiners looking for? And what marks will you get?

What will the exam paper look like?

There will be three questions on the paper:

(a) Compulsory: everyone has to do this.

(b) (i) and (b) (ii) You will have a choice here and will only have to answer one (b) question.

Sources   There will be nine sources on the examination paper. But don't worry: you won't have to deal with them all! You'll only need to deal with six sources – three for each of the questions you will be answering. And here is the good news. So far, you have worked with very long sources, some of which were complicated. In the examination, because you will only have one hour and twenty minutes to answer the two questions, the sources will be much shorter. You'll probably be dealing with no more than around 550 words altogether.

Question (a)

What will you have to do, and what marks will you get for doing it?

(a)   You will have to focus on reaching a judgement by analysis, cross-referencing and evaluation of source material. The maximum number of marks you can get is 20. You will be working at any one of four levels. Try to get as high up in the levels as you can. Remember that the only knowledge, outside of that which you can find in the sources, is what examiners call 'contextual' knowledge. This means you can write enough to enable you to interpret the source, but no more. For example, if one of the three sources is by Charles Parnell, you should show the examiners that you know he is the leader of the Irish Party, which is an organisation pressing for Home Rule, but you should not describe tactics of the Irish Party, nor the acts members carried out unless this information helps the understanding of a particular source.

Level 1

1–5 marks

Have you shown that you understand the surface features of the sources, and have you shown that you have selected material relevant to the question? Does your response consist mainly of direct quotations from the sources?

Level 2

6–10 marks

Have you identified points of similarity and difference in the sources in relation to the question asked? Have you made at least one developed comparison or a range of undeveloped ones? Have you summarised the information you have found in the sources? Have you noted the provenance of at least one of the sources?

Level 3

11–15 marks

Have you cross-referenced between the sources, making detailed comparisons supported by evidence from the sources? Have you shown that you understand you have to weigh the evidence by looking at the nature, origins, purpose and audience of the sources? Have you shown that you have thought about considering 'How far' by trying to use the sources as a set?

Level 4

16–20 marks

Have you reached a judgement in relation to the issue posed by the question? Is this judgement supported by careful examination of the evidence of the sources? Have you cross-referenced between the sources and analysed the points of similarity and disagreement? Have you taken account of the different qualities of the sources in order to establish what weight the evidence will bear? Have you used the sources as a set when addressing 'How far' in the question?

Now try this (a) question.

Study Sources A, B and C.

How far do Sources A and B challenge the proposals expressed in Source C?

Source A

From the very outset of our conversations I told you that we look to Ireland to own allegiance to the throne, and to make her future as a member of the British Commonwealth. That was the basis of our proposals, and we cannot alter it. The status which you claim in advance for your delegates is in effect a repudiation of that basis. I must therefore repeat that unless the second paragraph in your letter of 12 September is withdrawn, conference between us is impossible.

Part of a letter written by David Lloyd George to Éamon de Valera on 18 September 1921

Source B

I proposed another way out – external association of Ireland with the group of free nations in the British Empire. In entering such an association Ireland would be doing nothing incompatible with her declared independence. This proposal in its main outline was accepted by the [Dáil] Cabinet and the whole Ministry (about 15 members were present when I made it) and I set out with the fixed determination of making peace on that basis.

Part of a letter written by Éamon de Valera to fellow Republican Joseph McGarrity on 21 December 1921

Source C

Ireland will agree to be associated with the British Commonwealth for all purposes of common concern, including defence, peace and war, and political treaties, and to recognise the British Crown as Head of the Association. The Oath to be taken by members of the Irish Parliament shall be in the following form: I do swear to bear true faith and allegiance to the Constitution of Ireland and to the Treaty of Association of Ireland with the British commonwealth of Nations, and to recognise the King of Great Britain as Head of the Associated States.

Amendments proposed to the Treaty of London by the Irish Delegates, 4 December 1921

Now use the marking criteria to assess your response.

How did you do?

What could you have done to have achieved a better mark?

Question (b)

What will you have to do and what marks will you get for doing it?

(b) You will have to analyse and evaluate a historical view or claim using two sources and your own knowledge. There are 40 marks for this question. You will get 24 marks for your own knowledge and 16 marks for your source evaluation. You can be working at any one of four levels.

Try to get as high up in the levels as you can. The examiners will be marking your answer twice: once for knowledge and a second time for source evaluation.

This is what the examiners will be looking for as they mark the ways in which you have selected and used your knowledge to answer the question:

Level 1

1–6 marks

Have you written in simple sentences without making any links between them? Have you provided only limited support for the points you are making? Have you written what you know separately from the sources? Is what you have written mostly generalised and not really directed at the focus of the question? Have you made a lot of spelling mistakes and is your answer disorganised?

Level 2

7–12 marks

Have you produced a series of statements that are supported by mostly accurate and relevant factual material? Have you make some limited links between the statements you have written? Is your answer mainly 'telling the story' and not really analysing what happened? Have you kept your own knowledge and the sources separate? Have you made a judgement that isn't supported by facts? Is your answer a bit disorganised with some spelling and grammatical mistakes?

Level 3

13–18 marks

Is your answer focused on the question? Have you shown that you understand the key issues involved? Have you included a lot of descriptive material along with your analysis of the issues? Is your material factually accurate but a bit lacking in depth and/or relevance? Have you begun to integrate your own knowledge with the source material? Have you made a few spelling and grammatical mistakes? Is your work mostly well organised?

Level 4

19–24 marks

Does your answer relate well to the question focus? Have you shown that you understand the issues involved? Have you analysed the key issues? Is the material you have used relevant to the question and factually accurate? Have you begun to integrate what you know with the evidence you have gleaned from the source material? Is the material you have selected balanced? Is the way you have expressed your answer clear and coherent? Is your spelling and grammar mostly accurate?

This is what the examiners are looking for as they mark your source evaluation skills.

Level 1

1–4 marks

Have you shown that you understand the sources? Is the material you have selected from them relevant to the question? Is your answer mostly direct quotations from the sources or re-writes of them in your own words?

Level 2

5–8 marks

Have you shown that you understand the sources? Have you selected from them in order to support or challenge from the view given in the question? Have you used the sources mainly as sources of information?

Level 3

9–12 marks

Have you analysed the sources, drawing from them points of challenge and/or support for the view contained in the question? Have you developed these points, using the source material? Have you shown that you realise you are dealing with just one viewpoint and that the sources point to other, perhaps equally valid ones? Have you reached a judgement? Have you supported that judgement with evidence from the sources?

Level 4

13–16 marks

Have you analysed the sources, raising issues from them? Have you discussed the viewpoint in the question by relating it to the issues raised by your analysis of the source material? Have you weighed the evidence in order to reach a judgement? Is your judgement fully explained and supported by carefully selected evidence?

Now try this (b) question.

Read Sources D, E and F and use your own knowledge.

Do you agree with the view, hinted at in Source F, that Gladstone's proposal for Home Rule was driven by a desire for parliamentary tranquillity [peace]?

Source D

Downing Street. Long interview for 2 hours with Mr Gladstone at his request . . . As to a Dublin Parliament, I argued that he was making a surrender all along the line. A Dublin Parliament would work with constant friction, and would press against any barrier he might keep to keep up the unity of the 3 kingdoms. I told him to get rid of the Irishmen from Westminster, such as we have known them for 5 or 6 years past, would do something to make his propositions less offensive and distasteful in Great Britain tho' it tends to separation. I thought he placed far too much confidence in the leaders of the Rebel Party. I could place none in them and the general feeling was and is that any terms with them would not be kept.

From the diary of John Bright written on 20 March 1886

Source E

In January 1881 a Fenian bomb had injured three people in Salford (Manchester); an unexploded bomb was found in the Mansion House in March; and again in May of the following year. In 1883 bombs exploded in Glasgow and London, and the next year four London railway stations were closed because terrorists, Irish conspirators, attempted to blow up London Bridge, and the newly opened Underground Railway was closed by bombers . . . It was against this background of anarchic violence that we are to understand Mr Gladstone's conversion to Home Rule for Ireland. The timing of the 'Hawarden Kite', was perhaps designed to cheer up the Irish voters, and to flush out the Tories as proponents of coercion: that is forcing tenant farmers to either pay their rents or take to the hedgerows. But it was a bold move, the beginning of the boldest and noblest phase and aspect of Gladstone's career.

Adapted from A.N. Wilson *The Victorians*, published in 2002

Source F

All Mr Gladstone's policy . . . since 1880 has been a policy of concession to the party of Mr Parnell, to weaken the power of the Loyalists and strengthen that of the disloyal party . . . If political parties and political leaders . . . should be so utterly lost to every feeling and dictate of honour and courage as to hand over coldly, and for the sake of purchasing a short and illusory Parliamentary tranquillity, the lives and liberties of the Loyalists of Ireland to their hereditary and bitter foes, make no doubt on this point – Ulster will not be a consenting party; Ulster at the proper moment will resort to . . . force: Ulster will fight, Ulster will be right . . .

From a speech to Unionists by Lord Randolph Churchill, Ulster Hall, Belfast, 22 February 1886

Now use the marking criteria to assess your response.

How did you do?

What could you have done to have achieved higher marks? ·

The examiners will not be nit-picking their way through your answer, ticking things off as they go. Rather, they will be looking to see which levels best fit the response you have written to the question, and you should do the same when assessing your own responses.

How will I time my responses?

You have 1 hour 20 minutes to answer two questions. Remember that the (a) question is compulsory and that you will have a choice of one from two (b) questions. Take time, say, five minutes, to read through the paper and think about your choice of (b) question. The (a) question is worth half the marks of the (b) question, so you should aim to spend twice the time on the (b) question. This means that, including planning time, you should spend about 25 minutes on the (a) question and about 50 minutes (again, including planning) on the (b) question.

You have now had a lot of practice in planning, writing and assessing your responses to the sort of questions you can expect to find on the examination paper. You are well prepared and you should be able to tackle the examination with confidence.

Good luck!

References

Andrews, C.S. (*c.*1979) *Dublin Made Me*, Mercier

Anonymous (1866) *The New York Times*, 26 October

Anonymous (1867) *Freeman's Journal*, 19 September

Anonymous (1880) *The Times*, 18 October

Anonymous (1885) *The Times*, 22 January

Anonymous (1921) Article in *Irish News*, 8 December

Atholl, Duke of (1918) 'Report on the Present State of Ireland, Especially with Regard to Conscription', unpublished report, 29 April

Barry, T. (1962) *Guerrilla Days in Ireland*, Anvil Books

Beckett, H.W. (ed.) (1986) *The Army and the Curragh Incident, 1914*, Bodley Head for the Army Records Society

Blunt, W. (1919) *My Diaries: Being a Personal Narrative of Events 1888–1914*, Martin Secker

Boycott, Captain (1880) Letter submitted to *The Times*, 18 October

Bright, J. Extract from diary, 20 March 1886.

Brugha, C. (1922) Speech to the Dáil, 7 January

Butt, I. (1870) *Home Government for Ireland. Irish Fundamentalism! Its Meaning, its Objects, and its Hopes*, Irish Home Rule League

Carlyle, T. (1837) *The French Revolution: A History*, James Fraser

Carlyle, T. (1839) *Chartism*, James Fraser

Cary, E. (1904) 'Review of *Ireland in the New Century* by Horace Plunkett', *New York Times*, 2 April

Chamberlain, J. (1885) *The Irish Question*, S. Sonnenschein & Co.

Christian Herald (1866) Drawing of Gladstone

Churchill, Lord R. (1866) Speech to Unionists, Ulster Hall, Belfast, 22 February

Churchill, W. (1913) Letter to John Redmond, 31 August

Collins, M. (1921) Letter to John O'Kane, 6 December

Connolly, J. (1916) 'Notes From The Front: The Ties That Bind', 5 February

Cooke, H. (1841) Speech made in Belfast, 22 January

Cowan, J. (1886) Speech in the House of Commons, *Hansard*, May

Craig, Capt. C. (1920) Speech to the House of Commons, *Hansard*, 29 March

Cummins, N. (1846) *The Times*, 24 December

Cusack, M. (1884) 'A Word About Irish Athletics', *The Irishman*, 11 October

Davitt, M. (1904) *The Fall of Feudalism in London*, Harper & Bros

de Valera, É. (1921) Letter to Joseph MacGarrity, 21 December

Devoy, J. (1878) Telegram to Charles Stewart Parnell, 25 October

Dicey, A.V. (1886) *England's Case Against Home Rule*, J. Murray

Dillon, J. (1909) 'Speech to the National Convention', *Weekly Freeman's Journal*, 20 February

Dillon, J. (1916) Speech to House of Commons, 16 May

Doris, W. (1916) Letter to John Redmond, 8 March

Encyclopaedia of World History, (1952) Houghton Mifflin

Ferriter, D. (2004) *The Transformation of Ireland, 1900–2000*, Overlook Press

Foster, R.F. (1988) *Modern Ireland 1600–1972*, Penguin

Foster, R.F. (1999) *Ireland 1798–1998*, Blackwell

George, D.L. (1919) Speech to the House of Commons, *Hansard*, 22 December

George, D.L. (1921) Letter to Éamon de Valera, 24 June

George, D.L. (1921) Letter to Éamon de Valera, 18 September

George, D.L. (1921) Letter to Éamon de Valera, 29 September

Gladstone, W. (1868) Speech in an election meeting in Lancashire

Gladstone, W. (1886) Speech in the House of Commons, 8 April

Gladstone, W. (1890) Letter to John Morley, 24 November

Ó Gráda, C. (1994) *Ireland: A New Economic History, 1780–1939*, OUP

Griffith, A. (1904) Article in *United Irishman*, 2 January

Griffith, A. (1917) Article in *Cork Examiner*, 26 October

Hepburn, D. (1834) 'O'Connell's speech to the House of Commons', 22 April, p. 15

Major, P. (1914) Howell, Letter to friend, Curragh Camp, 22 March

Hume, D. *History of England (1974–1762)*, NBTOS

Hyde, D. (1892) 'The Necessity for De-Anglicising Ireland', 25 November

Illustrated London News (1880) 'Departure of the Boycott Relief Volunteers From Lough Mask House', Mayo, 4 December

Illustrated London News (1916) 'Saying What They Think of Treason at Home', Easter issue

Irish Delegates (1921) Amendments to Treaty of London, 4 December

Irish Republican Army (1919) 'An t-Oglach', 31 January

Irish Volunteers (1914) Manifesto, 24 September

Jackson, A. (1999) *Ireland 1798–1998*, Blackwell

Jackson, A. (2004) *Home Rule – An Irish History 1800–2000*, Oxford University Press

Jackson, A. (1820) *Irish Ballad*, p. 27, publisher unknown

Jackson, A. (1828) *The Duke of Wellington*, p. 35, publisher unknown

Jenkins, R. (1997) *Gladstone: A Biography*, Random House

Jeudwine, Lieutenant-General Sir H. (1922) *Record of the Rebellion in Ireland in 1920–1921 and the Part Played by the Army in Dealing With it*, publisher unknown

Jones, T. (1921) Letter to Lloyd George, 5 December

Keating, S. (1921) *Men of the South*, publisher unknown

Kee, R. (1972) 'Ourselves Alone', in *The Green Flag: The Turbulent History of the Irish National Movement*, Delacorte Press

Kickham, C. (1865) Article published in the *Irish People*, 16 September

Kipling, R. (1912) *Ulster 1912*, Poem

Lalor, J.F. (1848) Letter to *The Irish Felon*, 24 June

Law, A.B. (1912) Speech at Blenheim Palace, *The Times*, 29 July

Law, A.B. (1914) Resolution of the Shadow Cabinet, 4 February

Law, H. (1918) *Contemporary Review*, June

London Illustrated Times (1848) 'Images of Irish tenants being evicted in 1840s', 16 December

Long, W. (1910) Speech to Ulster Unionist Council, Belfast, *The Times*, 5 January

Low, D. (1921) *What's In a Name*, publisher unknown

Lyons, F.S.L. (1971) *Ireland Since the Famine*, Weidenfeld & Nicolson

Macaulay, T.B. (1853) *History of England*, Pesten

Marx, K. (1867) Letter to Friedrich Engels, 14 December

MacCarthy, J. (1886) Speech in the House of Commons, *Hansard*, May

MacEntee, S. (1921) Speech on Dáil debate, 22 December

MacNeill, E. (1913) Article in *An Claidheamh Soluis*, 1 November

MacSwiney, M. (1917) Letter to Count Plunkett, May

Meagher, T.F. (1846) 'The Sword Speech', 28 July

Merry, T. (1886) 'The Home Rule Leap', *St Stephen's Review*, 4 September

Merry, T. (1889) 'Balfour Rescues Erin', *St Stephen's Review*, 16 March

Merry, T. (1896) *Lightning Artist Drawing Mr Gladstone*, film

Merry, T. (1869) *Sketching Lord Salisbury*, film

Miles, Second Lieutenant E.G. (1914) Letter to his father, 21 March

Mitchel, J. (1854) 'The New York Citizen', *Jail Journal*

Mitchel, J. (1861) *The Last Conquest of Ireland (Perhaps)*, publisher unknown

Morgan, D.P. (1901) *The Leader*, 27 July

Morgan, M. (1869) 'The Irish Frankenstein', *The Tomahawk*, 18 December

National Library of Ireland (1914) Minutes from the Buckingham Palace Conference, July

O'Brien, R.B. (1883) *Life of Charles Stewart Parnell 1846–1891*, Harper

O'Connor, F. (1958) *An Only Child*, Knopf

O'Malley, E. (1936) *On Another Man's Wound*, Rich & Cowan

Owen, W.H. (1916) Report to Lloyd George, June

Pall Mall Gazette (1885) 'Hawarden Kite', 17 December

Parnell, C.S. (1876) Address to the House of Commons, *Hansard*, 30 June

Parnell, C.S. (1880) Article from *The Times*, 20 September

Parnell, C.S. (1882) 'The Irish Frankenstein', in *The Works of C.S. Parnell*, *Punch*, 20 May

Parnell, C.S. (1886) 'Second Reading of the Irish Home Rule Bill', *The Times*, 8 June

Parnell, C.S. (1887) Article from *The Times*

Partridge, B. (1920) 'The Kindest Cut of All', *Punch*, 10 March

Pearse, P. (1914) Article in *Irish Freedom*

Pearse, P. (1916) *The People Who Wept at Gethsemane*, March

Pearse, P. (1916) James Connolly and Horace Plunkett, *Declaration of the Irish Republic*, 24 April

Pictorial Times (1846) 'Food Riot in Dungarvan', 10 October

Plunkett, H. (1904) 'Ireland in the New Century', *New York Times*, 2 April

Power, E.G. (1988) *Modern Ireland*, Longman

Proctor, J. (1884) 'Orange and Fenian', *Moonshine*, 12 January 1884.

Punch (1882) 'The Irish Frankenstein, 20 May

Punch (1916) 'Wanted – A St Patrick', May

Punch (1921) 'The Problem Play', Summer

Punch Almanac (1893) 'Home Rule: Ulster Last Ditch', April

Redmond, J. (1911–1912) *Their Irish Master*, Postcard

Redmond, J. (1913) Speech to Irish Nationalists, Limerick, 12 October

Redmond, L. (1914) Speech to Irish Volunteers, Woodenbridge, Wicklow, 20 September

Rigney, F. (1916) 'Erin's Tragic Easter', illustration

Salisbury, Lord (1996) Speech in the House of Lords, *Hansard*, 4 June

Shawe-Taylor, Cpt. J. (1902) Open Letter of Irish Newspapers, September

Sinn Féin (1918) Manifesto to the Irish People, December

Somerville-Large, P. (2000) *Irish Voices: An Informal History 1916–1966*, 2nd edn, Pimlico

Stott, W.R.S. (1920) 'Sinn Féin Murder of an Army Officer at Dublin', *The Illustrated London News*, 11 December

Swain, J. (1890) 'Gladstone and Parnell', *Punch*, December

Tenniel, J. (1866) 'The Fenian Pest', *Punch*

Tenniel, J. (1867) 'The Fenian Guy Fawkes', *Punch*, 28 December

Tenniel, J. (1881) 'The Land Act is Handed to Hibernia', *Punch*, 13 August

Tenniel, J. (1881) 'Time Waxworks', *Punch*, 31 December

Tenniel, J. (1886) 'An Exit Speech', *Punch*, 22 May

The Times (1846) Newspaper editorial, 22 September

The Tomahawk (1867) 'Fenian Dragon Defeating St George', unattributed illustration

Ulster Bank (1863) Circular, Ulster Bank

Ulster Unionist Council (1904) Resolution passed at preliminary meeting, Belfast, 2 December

Vaughan, W.E. (1975) 'Landlords and Tenants in Ireland in 1848–1904', *Studies in Irish Economic and Social History*, Number 2

Walsh, Archbishop (1885) *United Ireland*, 21 November

The Weekly Freeman (1887) 'In the Lion's Den,' 23 July

Whitehall Review (1885) 'Forgotten', May

Yeats, W.B. (1916) *Easter 1916*

Yeats, W.B. (1918) Letter to Lord Haldane, May

Glossary of key terms

AOH Stands for Ancient Order of Hibernians. It was set up in 1836 in the United States of America to protect the interests of the Catholics. In Ireland, the AOH became strongly linked to the Irish Party

Ard-fheis A party conference

Black and Tan A nickname that came from the uniforms worn by newly recruited soldiers. They wore dark green RIC caps and tunics with khaki trousers. This reminded people of the uniform of a famous hunt from Limerick of the same name

The Boer War A colonial war fought between Britain and the Boer provinces of the Orange Free State and Transvaal Republic. The Boers were the descendents of Dutch settlers and they resented the spread of British rule

Brunswick Clubs Formed in the heat of the debate about Catholic Emancipation in 1827–28, the Brunswick Clubs stood firmly against any concession to the Catholics

Calvary Where Jesus was crucified

Catholic Association Initially set up by Daniel O'Connel as a middle-class based organisation in 1823, it was turned into a mass movement by the introduction of the 'Catholic Rent', the contribution to the Association of a penny a month. Money raised was used to help fund election campaigns for Association candidates as well as supporting Association members who had been evicted from their homes

Catholic Emancipation This would involve giving Catholics the same rights of representation and civil liberties as enjoyed by Protestants

Clan na Gael Means 'family of the Gaels' (a Gael is someone who speaks Gaelic). It was set up in 1867 as a rival organisation to the Fenian Brotherhood, which was eventually replaced by the 1870s as the dominant voice of Fenianism in the United States of America

Commutation The process of reducing a sentence to a less severe one

Coupon Election In the run up to the General Election of 14 December 1918, the 159 Liberal candidates supporting Lloyd George were sent a joint letter of backing from Lloyd George and Andrew Bonar Law, leader of the Conservative Party. It was Asquith who nicknamed the letter a 'coupon' (there was still rationing at the time)

Cultural revival This term is used to describe the period towards the end of the nineteenth century when there was a renewed interest in Irish culture from the Irish language to Irish sports. Many groups were founded during this period in order to promote Irish activities, most notably the Gaelic Athletic Association (GAA).

Dáil Éireann The Irish Parliament

Defence of the Realm Act 1914   An Act passed by the House of Commons as an emergency wartime measure in August 1914. Included in its measures were the right of the state to imprison people without trial

Diaspora   The dispersal of a people around the world and away from their original homeland. The Irish Diaspora saw the Irish move in large numbers to Britain and North America but also to Australia and New Zealand

Disestablishment   An established Church is when it is the official Church of state and receives support from the state. Disestablishment is when the status of a Church as the official Church of a state is removed

Dominion Status   The status held by other established members of the Empire, such as Canada and Australia. It meant that they were self governing but still had the British monarch as Head of State

Dublin Castle   The castle was the administrative heart of British rule in Ireland. It was where the Chief Secretary and civil service were based

Fenian   A nickname for a member of an organisation known as the Irish Republican Brotherhood, which was set up by James Stephen and John O'Mahony in 1858 to fight British rule in Ireland. A Fenian in the middle ages and before was an Irish warrior

The Four Courts   The Four Courts were highly significant as the centre of Ireland's legal system. It was where Dublin's main courts were situated and where the records were kept

Frankenstein's monster   Fenianism and the Irish in general were depicted as Frankenstein's monster. A favourite of Victorians, it refers to the creature at the heart of Mary Shelley's Gothic novel

Freemasons   People who belong to a secret international organisation, which promotes mutual help between members. Freemason meetings follow distinct ritual and their belief in a Supreme Being rather than the Christian God brought Freemasons into bitter conflict with the Catholic Church

Gethsamane   This is the garden where, according to the Bible, Jesus and his disciples withdrew to pray after the last supper and the night before Jesus's crucifixion

Grattan's Parliament   The name given to the Irish Parliament, which sat in the two decades up to the Act of Union in 1801

Habeas corpus   A basic human right which demands that anyone who is arrested must be brought to court to prove that he or she has a case to answer, or be released

Hansard   The published record of what is said in Parliament. From 1829 and 1909, *Hansard* was in private hands but became an ever more reliable record as the nineteenth century progressed. From 1907, *Hansard* was produced by Parliament as the official record of proceedings

Hawarden Kite   The term to 'fly a kite' is used in politics when a politician raises an idea via the media with the intention of gauging reaction to that idea. Hawarden was the name of Gladstone's home

Home Rule   This involved the devolution of some powers to an Irish Assembly in which decisions would be made about Irish affairs

House of Correction   A House of Correction was where petty criminals would be put to hard labour in an attempt to reform their criminal ways. The aims were to reform as well as punish

Hurling   A game played with sticks called hurleys and a ball. The aim of the game is to hit the ball into a goal for three points or between two posts for one point

Laissez faire The dominant political and economic philosophy for most of the first half of the nineteenth century. It revolved around the belief that the government should interfere as little as possible, thereby allowing the natural laws of economics to function

Lock-Out This was when employers lock their factories to prevent their workers from coming to work

Moratorium Another word for a delay or temporary suspension

'Ne plus ultra' The translation from Latin, 'no more beyond' (a certain point). In this context it means the ultimate goal of Irish nationalism

Non-clerical A group which is not influenced by the Catholic Church

Non-conformism Belonging to a church other than the established Church of Ireland

Non-sectarian An organisation which is open to people from different faiths or groups. In the context of Fenianism and Irish history generally, groups which are non-sectarian hope to appeal to Catholics and Protestants

Orangeism The Orange Order was founded in 1795 to defend Protestantism in Ireland. For the first half of the nineteenth century it was identified with rowdy and violent behaviour. It gained a broad popular basis from the 1880s in rejection of the Land League and then Home Rule

Orange Order Named after King William III of Orange who had successfully defeated the Catholic forces of James II at the Battle of the Boyne in 1689, thereby ensuring the Protestant Ascendancy

Papist Another word used to describe a Catholic (usually disparaging)

Paramilitary A paramilitary force is an unofficial military organisation

Peace Conference The Peace Conference referred to in Sinn Féin's manifesto was the Versailles Conference, which met at the end of the First World War. American President Woodrow Wilson's proposals, known as the Fourteen Points, suggested that all peoples should be able to determine, through democracy, their nation state

The Poor Law The means of helping the poor in Britain and Ireland. Relief was given inside a workhouse or through what was called 'outdoor relief', i.e. allowances given to supplement the wages of the poor living in the community

Presbyterians Protestants whose church was run in a different way to the Churches of England or Ireland. They did not recognise the British monarch as their head, nor did they believe in bishops. Because they, and other Protestant groups such as the Quakers, did not conform to the rules of the established Church of England and Ireland, they were called non-conformists

Protective Tariffs Taxes imposed on imports. Such taxes would benefit Irish agriculture but not industry

Punch magazine A magazine set up in 1841 by Henry Mayhew. Within a decade it had become very popular, especially amongst the middle classes because it was sophisticated rather than rude in its humour

Reformed Parliament In 1832, the Great Reform Act had changed the composition of Parliament by giving the vote to the middle classes. It also removed some of the more corrupt aspects of the previous electoral system such as rotten boroughs, which were constituencies with hardly any voters

Satire The use of humour or irony to make a point

Second Reading   The most important stage in the passage of a piece of legislation through Parliament. At the Second Reading stage, the proposed law is debated by the House of Commons and Lords and then voted on

Secular   The opposite of clerical. A secular university is one which is not based on religion

Sedition   A charge laid against those people whose words or deeds are said to undermine monarch or state

Social deference   This is when people will show respect to others because of their class rather than because of who they actually are

Trinity College, Dublin   Founded in 1592 by Queen Elizabeth I. Throughout the eighteenth century, it acted as part of the Protestant Ascendancy but Catholics were admitted in 1793. It remained an important part of Protestant culture throughout the nineteenth and early twentieth centuries

Ulster Special Constabulary   The USC was created in October 1920. There were three types of Special Constables: the most infamous were the part-timers known as the B-specials. The USC often used violence and intimidation against the nationalist community and were highly effective

Umbrella movement   An umbrella movement is a movement that includes a number of viewpoints

Whig   A political grouping in Britain which stood for the power of Parliament and limited powers of the Crown. Their opponents were the Tories who stood for maintaining the established political order

Index

Page references in *italics* indicate illustrations.